IAN CARRADICE

# GREEK COINS

Published for the Trustees of the British Museum
by British Museum Press

IN MEMORIAM
Martin Jessop Price
1939–1995

© 1995 The Trustees of the British Museum

Published by British Museum Press
A division of The British Museum Company Ltd
46 Bloomsbury Street, London WC1B 3QQ

ISBN 0–7141–2210–6

A catalogue record for this book is available from
the British Library

Designed by Andrew Shoolbred
Cover designed by Grahame Dudley Associates

Photoset in Garamond No. 3 by
Rowland Phototypesetting Ltd, Bury St Edmunds, Suffolk
Printed in Great Britain by
The Bath Press, Avon

*Front cover:* Detail of reverse of silver stater of Heraclea in South Italy, *c.* 330 BC,
depicting Heracles and the Nemean lion (fig. 31d).

*Frontispiece:* Head of Hera and head of Zeus, on silver staters of the Peloponnese,
4th century BC (fig. 26b, a).

# Contents

# Preface

The purpose of this book is to present a history of Greek coinage, century by century, from its origins in the Lydian region of Asia Minor in the late seventh century BC to the conquest of the Hellenistic kingdoms by Rome in the first century BC. The influence of ancient Greek coinage through to modern times is also outlined in the final chapter. The survey of Greek coinage by centuries 'before Christ' is clearly artificial, since the ancient Greeks could have had no sense of belonging to a period of a hundred years within a counting scheme devised long after their time. It would also be a mistake to assume that developmental trends can always be time-linked in a world as large and, in terms of both politics and culture, as diverse as that of the ancient Mediterranean. However, artificial though it may be, the division of pre-Christian history into centuries at least provides a convenient temporal structure in which to place events and developments and thus to facilitate their understanding.

In the survey, and in its illustrations, the book concentrates on precious metal coinage, especially issues of the larger-denomination silver coins. This inevitably leads to huge under-representation of lower-value coinages, especially Greek bronze coins, which were produced in abundance, especially from the fourth to the first centuries. A comprehensive catalogue would have to include much more bronze coinage, but here the purpose is to describe and illustrate the evolution of Greek coinage and how it reflects Greek history, art and society. As only a small sample of the enormous and diverse range of issues can be shown, the focus must be on the best-made and best-preserved pieces, which are invariably those minted in precious metals. Although a limited amount of information and comment can be provided in a book of this length, the inclusion of a good number of illustrations of gold and silver coins allows some of the finest examples of Greek numismatic art to be seen. These are the coins that have excited collectors and scholars over the ages, and continuing study of them will no doubt yield new insights in the future.

In the text are frequent references to literary and epigraphic evidence for coins. The selection of references has been made much easier since the recent publication by John Melville Jones, *Testimonia Numaria: Greek and Latin Texts concerning Ancient Greek Coinage* (vol. 1, London, 1993), whose translations of texts and inscriptions have been used. References to this work have been abbreviated to *TN*. The other abbreviations used are *IG*: *Inscriptiones Graecae* (Berlin, 1873–); *OGIS*: *Orientis Graeci Inscriptiones Selectae* (ed. W. Dittenberger, Leipzig, 1903–5); *SIG*: *Sylloge Inscriptionum Graecorum* (ed. W. Dittenberger, Leipzig, 1915–24); *P. Petrie*: *The Flinders Petrie Papyri* (ed. J. P. Mahaffy and J. G. Smyly, Dublin, 1891–1905); *P. Eleph. Elephantine Papyri* (ed. O. Rubensohn, Berlin, 1907).

This book necessarily owes a debt to many previous works in the subject area, including *TN* and some of the other books listed under Further Reading. I also wish to mention some of the individuals who have helped in the production of this volume. Nina Shandloff of British Museum Press has been a patient and supportive editor, and in the Department of Coins and Medals Andrew Burnett, Ute Wartenberg and Janet Larkin have provided much needed intellectual or practical assistance. The fact that all of the items illustrated in this book are in the collections of the British Museum serves to emphasise the key contribution made by that institution.

Finally, I would like to mention my former colleague at the British Museum, Martin Price, whose help and encouragement in past years provided the foundation for much of my work on Greek coins. Martin Price will rightly be remembered for the great contributions he made to numismatic scholarship, through works such as his catalogue of *The Coinage in the Name of Alexander the Great and Philip Arrhidaeus* (Zurich/London, 1991), but he was also keen to advance the popularisation of Greek numismatics, and the enthusiasm he showed for his chosen subject was an inspiration to many. This book is therefore dedicated to the memory of Martin Price.

# CHAPTER 1

# Coinage and the Ancient Greek World

G reek coins survive today as small but durable relics of the ancient civilisations which produced them. They provide a physical link with a distant past that is special because our modern coins are their direct descendants. They thus have an instant familiarity through their resemblance to everyday objects of our own time, yet they are tinged with a special aura given by their obvious preciousness and great antiquity, not to mention their artistic qualities and possible historic associations. Surviving silver coins from Athens dating from the fifth century BC are as much a product of the 'Classical Age' of Greece as the Parthenon, whose builders could themselves have handled these very coins. And few people today would be unmoved by the sight of a tray of gleaming gold and silver coins of Alexander the Great with labels identifying mints in cities like Ephesus, Tyre, Memphis and Babylon. These coins can conjure up images of a famous Greek hero and of fabulous Persian wealth turned into booty through military conquest.

Just as there are famous ancient Greek sites and personalities, there are also Greek coins which have become familiar. When Greek coins are used as illustrative material in history books, for television programmes on ancient history/civilisation, in advertisements (from book clubs to Greek holidays), we tend to see the same recurring images: the owl of the Athenian tetradrachm (four-drachma silver coin), the four-horse chariots or head of Arethusa on the magnificent coins of Syracuse, the head of Heracles on the silver coins of Alexander the Great or the portrait of Alexander himself on coins of Lysimachus of Thrace, or perhaps the turtle or tortoise of Aegina or the winged horse (Pegasus) of Corinth.

These images are employed for immediate impact, whether it is because they are particularly apt, or just so visually striking.

We can use one of these familiar Greek coins to introduce some of the terms used by numismatists. The silver tetradrachm of Athens, minted in the mid-fifth century BC, has designs on both sides. The 'head' side is termed the obverse, the 'tail' side the reverse. The designs themselves are called types (from the Greek word τυπος, *typos,* meaning the imprint of a blow), and the letters or inscription are referred to as the legend (from the Latin *legere,* to read). The area around the main design is called the field, and in the field on the reverse of this coin there are, in addition to the legend, symbols (sprig of olive and crescent moon) which are adjuncts to the main type, the owl. If the coin has an area at the bottom of the field clearly separated from the rest, this is referred to as the exergue.

The Athenian tetradrachm of the fifth century BC is obviously an ancient Greek coin, but the term 'Greek' can equally be applied to coins produced in ancient times from as far afield as Spain, Russia, Egypt and India. The phrase 'Greek coins' has been used traditionally in numismatic study as a convenience simply to describe any coins that were not produced by the ancient Romans (Republic or Empire). Thus the 'Celtic' coins produced by the native inhabitants of Britain in the Iron Age appear in *Historia Numorum,* the definitive manual of ancient Greek coinage first published in 1887. Also included here are the coins of the Carthaginians, whether minted in North Africa, Spain or Italy, and the issues of the Persian Empire, the Parthians, the Hasmonaean and Herodian rulers of Judaea and many other eastern kingdoms. There is

1 *Silver tetradrachm of Athens, mid-5th century* BC, *depicting Athena and her owl.* (2 × *actual size*)

some sense in this, since coinage was essentially a Greek phenomenon which spread to all the many regions inhabited by Greeks, and when it was adopted by their non-Greek neighbours (including, incidentally, the Romans) it usually retained its 'Greek' physical characteristics. It is indeed difficult to define the boundaries between Greek and non-Greek and this is one of the fascinations of studying Greek coins, which, because of their great number and variety, provide a uniquely broad view of the ancient world.

## The making of Greek coins

'One may speak of striking coins, of putting a stamp upon them.'

(Julius Pollux, *Onomasticon* 3, 86)

Most Greek coins were manufactured by a process known as striking. The flan of metal for the coin was placed between two dies whose designs were transferred to the coin when the dies were hammered together.

The coins were often irregularly shaped, unlike modern machine-made pieces, but their weights were precise. According to Isidore of Seville, writing in the seventh century AD: 'In coinage three things are sought: metal, design and weight' (*Etymologiae* 16, 18). The required weight standard varied from place to place. For instance, in the fifth and fourth centuries BC the Aeginetan standard, with a silver stater of 12 g containing two drachmae of 6 g, was widely used in most of mainland Greece, the Aegean islands and Crete, while the Attic or Euboeic standard, with a tetradrachm of 17.2 g containing four drachmae of 4.3 g, was used by Athens and her allies, and in Euboea and Sicily. Corinth and her colonies in north-western Greece used the Corinthian stater of 8.6 g, containing three drachmae, and in South Italy a group of cities earlier colonised by Achaean Greeks from the Peloponnese used a stater of 8 g divided into three drachmae. Other weight standards were used in the East: the Rhodian tetradrachm of 15.3 g used by Chios and Rhodes and many other cities in the fourth century BC; the Persian or Lydian shekel or double siglos of 11 g and the Phoenician shekel of 14 g, used not only in Phoenicia but appearing also in Thrace and Macedonia. Alexander the Great adopted for his imperial coinage the Attic standard, which subsequently became dominant through much of the eastern Mediterranean and beyond. These various weight standards derived from pre-coinage weight systems, as did some of the coin terms — drachma = 'handful', stater and shekel = 'weighing' – and well after the invention of coinage the weights of metal continued to have significance. Ancient hoards have been found containing both coins and uncoined bullion, and some records show evidence of the weighing of coins, particularly for calculating the value of 'foreign' silver and gold coins.

The metal used for striking Greek coins came from a variety of sources. The earliest coins were made of white gold, a natural alloy of gold and silver which occurred in the Lydian region of Asia Minor. White gold can also be produced artificially by mixing gold and silver, when it is referred to as electrum. Silver and gold were mostly obtained through underground mining. Probably the most famous of all ancient Greek mines were those of Laurium in Attica, which yielded much of the silver used for striking Athenian coinage:

> Lauriotic owls will never leave you,
> but will dwell within and will nest in
> your purses and hatch out small change.

> (Aristophanes, *Birds*, 1105)

The Athenians were obtaining so much silver from the Laurium mines in the early fifth century BC that it was proposed to make a public distribution of the surplus, amounting to ten drachmae for every citizen. A leading statesman, Themistocles, successfully argued that the money should be spent on building warships instead.

The region to the north of the Aegean Sea was also rich in mineral ores for precious metals, enabling the tribes of Thrace and Macedonia to produce substantial silver coinages in the late sixth and fifth centuries BC and Philip II of Macedonia (359–336) to initiate a major gold coinage. Other famous mining areas in the ancient world included parts of Asia Minor and Spain and the Aegean island of Siphnos. Some areas, such as South Italy and Sicily, were not blessed with silver or gold mines, yet they still managed to produce great quantities of coinage, particularly in silver. This must have been obtained from the metal already in circulation, in the form of bullion, silver plate or existing coinage. Trade would obviously have provided a way of acquiring the necessary metal, but war booty, tribute, taxes and various other means could also have contributed. The Phocians who seized Delphi during the Sacred War (356–

346 BC) used the offerings from the sanctuary to make large quantities of coinage. The Phocian general, Phayllus, needing money for the recruitment of mercenaries and allies, is said to have 'struck coins from the 120 golden ingots dedicated by Croesus king of the Lydians . . . and from the 360 golden goblets . . . and from a golden lion and a woman' (Diodorus Siculus 16, 56, 6). His sacrilege was believed to have been the cause of his succumbing soon after to a 'lingering disease'. There are also stories of rulers calling in silver (in coin or other forms – plate, jewellery, and so on) from their citizens for restriking as new coin.

The design provides the defining characteristic of a coin. It distinguishes the coin from the unmarked metal nugget which can equally serve as money, but only after its value has been measured by weighing. The coin's design in principle removes the necessity for weighing because it gives the piece of metal an officially authorised value. It could be argued that the earliest coin designs are little more than punched impressions intended principally to expose the interior of the metal and thus to confirm its genuineness. They are not so different from the unmarked metal nuggets or ingots used as money for centuries before the invention of coinage. However, the early punches were soon equipped with designs, as also were the anvils on which the flans of metal were struck, and thus coins with designs on both sides were born.

Although its purpose was essentially utilitarian, coin design became, in the hands of many Greek die-engravers, a medium for the exercise of imagination and artistic skill. An immensely wide variety of subjects could represent the coin-issuing authority: deities or their familiar attributes (sometimes both), characters from myths and legends, local products or famous natural or even man-made features. Where the coining authority was vested in an individual, heraldic devices could be used, or, particularly during the monarchies of the Hellenistic period, portraits of kings and/or queens. Some coin designs were apparently chosen as a deliberate pun on the name of the city – for example, the rose (ροδος, *Rhodos*) at Rhodes or the wild parsley (σελινον, *Selinon*) at Selinus in Sicily. The great variety of coin types reflects the political make-up of the Greek world, with its numerous independent or semi-independent city-states. And although some issuing authorities retained their principal coin design unchanged over long periods (as the well-recognised 'badge' of the city or kingdom), there could also be variety within the coinage of a single state, sometimes on one side of the coin, sometimes on both sides.

The extraordinary artistic skill of Greek die-engravers has long been recognised. The high relief created from striking by deeply engraved dies gives ancient Greek coins a sculptural quality which is entirely lacking in modern machine-made coins, and the products of certain ancient mints are regarded as true masterpieces of miniature art. Although no die-engravers are mentioned in any ancient texts on Greek art, some were clearly recognised as great artists or craftsmen in their own time and were allowed to sign their work. They were also employed by more than one patron as the production of more elaborate, imaginative or beautiful coin designs became an expression of civic pride and perhaps an aspect of inter-city rivalry. Thus, for instance, we observe the engraver Euainetos working in various Greek cities in Sicily – Camarina, Catana and Syracuse – between *c.* 415 and 385.

17

We can also see that the ancient Greeks recognised the artistic quality of their coin designs by the fact that they sometimes deliberately chose to copy some of the most attractive varieties. Although we cannot know for sure the motivation behind the choice of a particular coin design, it is reasonable to suppose that, whereas the much-imitated owl of Athens may have been copied because of the fame of the original or simply its familiarity (for a remote eastern settlement it may have been the only prototype available), if a city chose to imitate an uncommon variety from a geographically distant and politically unconnected city, the reason may well have been its sheer visual attractiveness. No other obvious explanation exists for the appearance of the facing head of a nymph in Tarsus, Cilicia (south-eastern Turkey), in the 370s BC which clearly derives from the facing-head Arethusa design by the engraver Kimon on coins of Syracuse, Sicily, *c.* 410, or, even more remarkably, the three-quarter-facing head of Athena on coins of the Lycian dynast Zagaba *c.* 380, which copies a rare design on Syracusan coins by the artist Eukleidas *c.* 410. On the Lycian coin the mint name Antiphellus in tiny letters replaces the artist's name on the visor of Athena's helmet.

2

The die-engraver's job was to prepare the dies for striking coins. Other individuals involved in the process of coin production were the mint workers who prepared metal flans and actually struck the coins, the officials (usually referred to as 'magistrates') who supervised production

a

b

2 *Copying a coin design:*
(a) *silver tetradrachm of*
*Syracuse in Sicily signed by*
*the artist Eukleidas c. 410;*
(b) *silver stater of the*
*dynast Zagaba from Lycia*
*in Asia Minor, minted at*
*Antiphellus c. 380, with*
*the same Athena head design*
*copying the Syracusan coin.*
(2 × *actual size*)

and were responsible for ensuring quality and preventing fraud, and finally the government officials who made the decision to mint coins in the first place.

It is clear that all, or virtually all, ancient coinage was produced by the state. Although the presence of personal names and heraldic devices on some of the earliest Greek coins may suggest private production, it is likely that even in these cases the individual who authorised the minting was acting on behalf of the state. Otherwise the designs on the vast majority of Greek coins make it abundantly clear that they are the official products of the state.

There are various reasons why coinage may be required: for making state payments (including military costs), for receiving state income (such as taxes), for facilitating exchange within the state and external trade. Although ancient peoples (for instance, Egyptians and Phoenicians) had managed to conduct all these activities without coinage, they were made much easier with its invention. A state could in theory use any available coinage of acceptable metal and weight, and there are many examples of Greek coins being used outside their home regions. However, the supply of 'foreign' coinage could not be guaranteed or regulated as easily as home production, and also there are additional reasons why a state would wish to produce its own coinage: political reasons, as in declaring independence or civic/national pride, or for reasons of profit. One of the most explicit ancient statements on this subject comes from the city of Sestus on the Thracian side of the Dardanelles, where an inscription honouring a citizen called Menas, dating from the second century BC, records that the city resolved to make its own bronze coinage for two reasons: '. . . in order that the city's emblem might have currency, and the city might receive the profit which would accrue . . .' (*OGIS* 339, 44–5).

Menas was an official responsible for carrying out the decision of the citizens of Sestus to furnish themselves with their own coinage. The names of such officials often appear on Greek coins, especially in the Hellenistic and Roman periods, though only rarely does the title of the office also appear, so it is often difficult to know if the named official was directly responsible for the coinage issue or if he was the chief local magistrate of the time (definitely identified when preceded by the phrase ΕΠΙ . . . , meaning 'in the time of . . .').

Magistrates' names are rare on Greek coins before the fourth century BC. Earlier issues used inscriptions more sparingly; often they were restricted to the city's name, either in full or abbreviated (for example, Συρακοσιον, meaning 'of the Syracusans', or ΑΘΕ, for 'of Athens' or 'of the Athenians'). For coinages issued under the authority of a ruler, as opposed to a republican city-state, the name of the king would usually appear. This is especially noticeable in certain Hellenistic coinages, when extended royal names (including titles) could fill the fields of the large silver coins.

Whether their names appeared on the coinage or not, there would always have been officials responsible for ensuring that the accounts of the mint were properly kept, that the correct quantities of coinage were produced and that the coinage would be of the prescribed quality. Corruption and fraud were always possible in mint operations, so it was important that there was a responsible official like Menas who would 'preserve this position of trust piously . . . [and discharge] the appropriate responsibilities'.

## Coinage in use

The uses to which coins were put could be much more varied than the reasons for their production. They might have been used in state payments, exchanged for goods, hoarded as wealth, used for loans, returned to the state in tax payments, sent abroad as tribute, and so on. In the course of their ancient circulation coins were liable to be counterstamped to change or confirm their value or cut to test their silver purity and their ultimate destination may have been the melting pot, burial in the ground (in a grave or treasure), dedication in a sanctuary, or use as jewellery.

Explicit evidence for the use of coinage comes mainly from ancient literature or inscriptions. There are numerous scattered references to coinage; some examples should suffice to illustrate the range.

Military expenses provide probably the earliest literary reference to the use of coinage, in a payment for military service made by a Lydian king in the early sixth century BC to the lyric poet Alcaeus. There are numerous examples from later periods, many concerned with the payment of mercenaries, such as those led by the historian Xenophon: '. . . So if you come with us, you will be taking revenge on your enemy, and each of you will receive a Daric [a Persian gold coin] a month, each captain twice as much, and each general four times as much' (Xenophon, *Anabasis* 7, 6, 7). Coinage was also frequently used in 'diplomacy': '. . . [Tithraustes] sent Timocrates the Rhodian to Greece, giving him gold to the value of fifty talents of silver, and ordering him to try . . . to give it to the leaders in the cities on condition that they made war on the

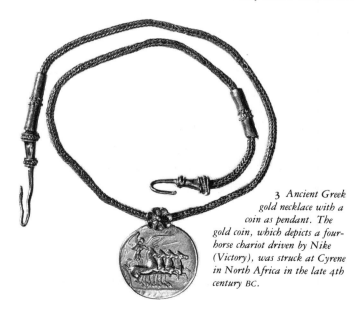

3 *Ancient Greek gold necklace with a coin as pendant. The gold coin, which depicts a four-horse chariot driven by Nike (Victory), was struck at Cyrene in North Africa in the late 4th century BC.*

Spartans' (Xenophon, *Hellenica* 3, 5, 1). When wars ended, more money changed hands as indemnity: '. . . the Carthaginians were to pay ten thousand talents over fifty years, delivering [to the Romans] two hundred Euboeic talents each year' (Polybius 15, 18, 7).

Coinage could obviously be used for exchange in payment of goods or labour: '. . . the horse which he [Xenophon] had bought at Lampsacus for fifty Darics' (*Anabasis* 7, 8, 6); 'This is the statue of Artemis; its price was two hundred Parian drachmas' (Diogenes Laertius 4.6 (*Arcesilaus*), 45). Other uses included taxes, fines, rewards, loans, marriage contracts, even magical charms: 'Memorandum from Cleon to Diotimus. I have been incorrectly assessed to the tax collector as owing for the vine tax of year 30, 90 drachmas' (*P. Petrie* II, xiii, 7); '. . . and anyone who disobeys and does not sit in his own division, is to be fined a stater . . .' (Samos, *SIG*³, 976); 'Anyone who denounces a conspiracy which is devised on Thasos, and is shown to be correct, is to receive a thousand staters from the city' (*TN* 396: from an inscription from Thasos); 'This man had lent him two thousand drachmas for the double voyage, on condition that he should be paid two thousand six hundred drachmas at Athens . . .' (Demosthenes, *Against Phormio* 23); '. . . let Heracleides repay to Demetria the dowry which she brought with her, a thousand drachmas, and let him pay a penalty in addition of a thousand drachmas of Alexander silver' (*P. Eleph.* 1, 11–12); 'What can one say of those who use spells and amulets, and bind bronze coins of Alexander the Macedonian on their heads and feet?' (St John Chrysostom, *Ad Illuminandos Catechesis* II, 5).

Finally there is the use of coins as savings and wealth. Inscriptions from religious sanctuaries, particularly in Athens, Delphi and Delos, include numerous references to coinage, especially lists of coins among the valuables in temple inventories, which give us important information on the currencies circulating in parts of the Greek world. Such information is also provided by the discoveries of coins buried in the ground, hoarding being the usual method of storing wealth in the days before banking. Numerous Greek coin hoards have been unearthed. Most of the Greek coins, especially in gold and silver, now in museum and private collections came from hoards, and not only are they a source of information on patterns of coinage production, output and circulation, they can also be used as evidence for private savings and wealth.

## CHAPTER 2

# Early Coinage and the Sixth Century

'Homer says that some made purchases with the skins of oxen,
others with iron or captives.'

(Pliny, *Natural History* 33, 3, 6–7)

Before the invention of coinage a wide variety of items was used
to express monetary values and to fulfil the functions which
were later mostly taken over by coined metal: exchange,
payment for services, hoarding of wealth and so on. The comment of
Pliny quoted above recalls a passage in the *Iliad* (Book 7, 472–5) where
Homer describes the Achaeans exchanging different commodities for
wine. It is therefore a reference dating from the eighth century BC
describing a Greek practice from earlier times that was no doubt still
prevalent. Anything which is recognised as having value can be used as
money, and from the earliest times to the present day various forms of
livestock, particularly cattle, have been used by so-called 'primitive'
peoples for this purpose. However, 'material' objects given value – for
instance, tools, vessels, pieces of metal or precious stones – have obvious
practical advantages, such as durability and portability, when compared
with cattle, and could be used for transactions even though their value
may still have been measured in terms of cattle. Thus in the *Iliad* (Book
23) a bronze cauldron is used as a sporting prize 'worth twelve oxen as
valued by the Achaeans'.

Lists of valuables kept in Greek temples include various vessels
(plates, cups, urns, bowls, jugs and so on) and objects relating to
sacrifices, including tripods, knives, axes and bundles of spits. Axes and,
especially, spits occur frequently in contexts suggesting their use as
money. Thus Herodotus (2, 135), writing in the fifth century BC,
describes the wealth of the prostitute Rhodopis which she sent as an

offering: '. . . she turned a tenth of her property into as large a number of ox-sized iron spits as this tithe would buy, and sent them to Delphi'. The ancient significance of spits as money was such that they were believed to have contributed to the vocabulary of coinage: 'As for the name of obols, some say that spits (*obeloi*) used for cooking beef were used for the purpose of exchange, and that the number of them which made a handful (*drax*) was called a drachma; and that these names, even when there was a change to the coinage which we now use, survived in memory of the ancient custom' (Julius Pollux, *Onomasticon* 9, 77).

Precious metals were highly valued, and long before the invention of coinage weighed quantities of silver were being used for monetary transactions by the ancient civilisations of the Near East in Egypt, the Levant and Mesopotamia. Stone or metal weights were used to regulate values and these have been found in archaeological excavations, along with the scales that were obviously needed to weigh the metal. The small nuggets of silver or gold thus used as money were the direct ancestors of coinage and because of the intrinsic value of precious metal they continued to be used after the invention of coinage, and indeed are often found alongside Greek coins in hoards.

## The invention of coinage

On the origins of coinage there are various questions that can be asked: What are the earliest coins? Where were they made and when? Who made them? Why were they made?

Information relating to some of these questions is provided by ancient writers, such as Julius Pollux:

> It would probably be thought over-ambitious to add to an account of coinage a discussion of the question whether Pheidon of Argos was the first to strike coins, or Demodice of Cyme, wife of the Phrygian Midas and daughter of Agamemnon king of Cyme, or the Athenians Erichthonius and Lycus, or the Lydians, as Xenophanes says, or the Naxians, which is the opinion of Aglaosthenes.      (*Onomasticon* 9, 83)

This passage from a Greek writer of the late second century AD indicates not only that the invention and early history of coinage were of interest to the ancients, but also that its origins were clouded with uncertainty and confused with legend. King Pheidon is recorded elsewhere as having struck (the first) silver coins in Aegina, *c.* 700 BC, but the tradition that the Lydians had an early involvement with coinage is backed up by the historian Herodotus who declared that the Lydians were 'the first people we know to have struck and used coinage of silver and gold' (1, 94).

Since there is no definitive, acceptable, documentary proof for the identity of the inventors of coinage, we must attempt to use the evidence provided by the coins themselves. The earliest coins of all are small electrum (white gold) pieces stamped with simple designs, and the most important evidence for their origin is provided by the site of the Temple of Artemis at Ephesus on the coast of Asia Minor (western Turkey). Here in 1904–5 archaeological excavations conducted by the British Museum unearthed nearly a hundred early electrum coins and coin-like objects. The simple stamped designs and the association with pre-coinage nuggets suggested to the excavators that they were witnessing the earliest evidence for the invention, and the archaeological circumstances of some of the finds, beneath the foundations of the mid-sixth-century Temple of Artemis, and the approximate dates of associated artefacts (jewellery, statuettes and so on) suggested a date for the deposits of no later than the early sixth century BC, perhaps earlier.

The 'coins' fell into different typological groups: unmarked silver or electrum nuggets; coins stamped on one side; coins stamped on one side and with rough patterns on the other side; coins combining stamps and proper designs (sometimes within rough patterns). These groups

b

4 *Early electrum coins:* (a) *the earliest known coin hoard, discovered in the foundations of the Temple of Artemis at Ephesus, probably buried as an offering to the goddess;* (b) *electrum stater attributed to Miletus in Ionia because the lion looking backwards became the standard design on later coins of the city.*

a

are thought to represent stages in the early development of coinage
('. . . one has the feeling of assisting at the very birth of coinage', wrote
the numismatist E. S. G. Robinson when studying the coins), though
the fact that they were all deposited together in unworn condition –
including a hoard of nineteen pieces in a pot – indicates that these stages 4
may have followed one another very rapidly and may even have over-
lapped.

Various different designs were included, mostly animals or animal-
parts, and some pieces were also inscribed with letters. These designs
and inscriptions, together with the location of finds, provide clues to the
identity of the coins' producers. The commonest types were coins with a
lion's head or paw. These are believed to be different denominations of
the same currency, and the likeliest issuer was the kingdom of Lydia, 6
since this was the major power in Asia Minor at the time and examples of
these coins are quite widespread elsewhere in the region. Other identifiable designs include a seal's head (attributed to the Ionian city of Phocaea
– φωκη = 'seal'), a recumbent lion (Miletus), and the forepart of a stag, 4
which is thought to be a fractional denomination of another coin which
depicts a grazing stag and carries the inscription: 'I am the badge of 5
Phanes'. The identity of this is uncertain, but a strong case has been
made for the city of Halicarnassus in Caria, since an example of the coin
type has been found there and the city later produced a mercenary leader
named Phanes. Other coin types from the Ephesus finds include
confronting figures of cocks, a goat's head, a horse's head, a beetle, a
griffin's head, a bull's head and a human head. Most cannot be
attributed. They do not correspond with later coin designs that can be
firmly attributed (like the seal from Phocaea or the lion from Miletus)
and it is quite possible that the designs are not the badges of cities at all,
but refer instead to local rulers, city officials or simply wealthy individuals. It is noticeable that the few inscriptions which can be deciphered all

5 *Electrum stater inscribed
with the name Phanes, from
an uncertain mint in Asia
Minor, c. 600 BC. (2 ×
actual size)*

seem to identify persons (Phanes, and Walwel and Kalil on Lydian lion-head pieces) rather than places.

It is reasonable to suppose that all the coin types represented in the excavation finds were produced not far from Ephesus, and that among them are the earliest of all coins, but we cannot be sure whether the very first coins were produced by Lydians or by the Greeks who had for centuries been settled in the coastal regions of Asia Minor. Agreement has yet to be reached concerning the date of these early coins, and new evidence might yet emerge to change current opinion, but the likeliest period for their production is the late seventh to early sixth centuries BC. Exactly why they suddenly appeared at this time remains a mystery. The stamping of pre-weighed nuggets of precious metal to validate their worth was a logical step to facilitate their circulation as money, but whether they were stamped primarily to act as a medium for making payments, for exchange in trade, for storing wealth, or for religious dedications (bearing in mind that the Ephesus finds were discovered in the foundations of a temple), or for some other reason, cannot yet be determined.

4

## Early gold and silver coins

The early electrum coinages all seem to have originated in Asia Minor. Not all were represented in the finds from Ephesus. The island of Samos produced a distinctive early series of electrum coinage to a heavier weight standard and with primitive abstract designs on the obverse. Another early producer was the city of Cyzicus to the north, whose coinages are all recognised by the presence of the city's badge of a tunny fish.

Electrum was probably chosen as the metal for the first coins because of its availability in the Lydian region, as the Lydian capital Sardes commanded the River Pactolus, which contained alluvial white gold. Since it was an alloy consisting of varying amounts of two metals of different worth (gold and silver), the intrinsic value of each electrum piece might differ, even when their weights were identical – hence the need to confirm value with a stamp. However, once the idea of stamped coinage had taken hold it was not surprising that it should soon spread to other metals. As we have seen, Herodotus believed that the Lydians were the first to use 'gold and silver coins', and the change to a bimetallic currency in Lydia is usually attributed to the time of King Croesus (*c.* 560–547 BC), a man whose name became synonymous with great wealth. The first Lydian gold and silver coins, which succeeded the lion-head electrum pieces, had designs with confronting foreparts of a lion and bull. It is generally assumed that these coins were introduced under Croesus, and the gold piece may in ancient times have been referred to as a 'Croeseid', though the evidence of hoards suggests that most, and possibly even all, of these issues were struck after the Lydian kingdom had been conquered by the Persians. Hoard evidence also shows that silver coinage spread from Lydia and Ionia into other parts of Asia Minor, with noticeably early issues apparently being produced to the south in Caria and Lycia.

6

6

The new practice also quickly extended into other more distant regions. It has been noted that the invention of coinage may have to be credited to the Lydians rather than the Greeks (though uncertainty remains). What cannot be doubted, however, is that the dramatic spread of silver coinage, starting in the mid-sixth century, was essentially a Greek phenomenon. By the end of the sixth century silver coins were being struck in the Aegean islands and the Greek mainland, to the north in Macedonia and Thrace, to the west in the Greek settlements in South Italy and Sicily, and to the east in the island of Cyprus and Cyrene on the north African coast. These were all areas inhabited by Greek-speaking peoples, whether they were long-established inhabitants, more recent colonists or traders. The rapid spread of coinage across such great distances was undoubtedly facilitated by the presence of Greek communities over such a wide area. Traditional teaching of Greek history may focus on the area of the present-day Greek state, and particularly on

6 *Early electrum and silver coins from Asia Minor, 6th century BC:* (a) *electrum third-stater of the Lydian kingdom, with the head of a lion;* (b) *Lydian silver 'Croeseid', with lion and bull design;* (c) *silver stater from Lycia with the forepart of a boar;* (d) *silver coin of Phocaea depicting a seal.*

a                 b                 c                 d

Athens, but we should remember that many famous ancient Greeks hailed from further afield: for example, Herodotus, the 'father of History', was from Halicarnassus in western Turkey; Pythagoras was born on the Aegean island of Samos but moved to Croton in southern Italy; Zeno, founder of the Stoic school of philosophy, originated from Citium in Cyprus; and Archimedes, the engineer of 'Eureka!' fame, was from Syracuse in Sicily. Because coinage eventually spread so comprehensively throughout all the areas of Greek influence, the surviving coins provide a useful reminder of the enormous geographical extent of the world of ancient Greek culture.

The earliest silver coins are not unlike the early electrum pieces, in that they tend to have designs on one side and punch marks on the other. Thus, for example, the early silver coins of each of the three main I, II producers in Greece in the later sixth century all share this characteristic, although they are otherwise quite different from each other. The early coins of the island of Aegina, where Pheidon was supposed to have inaugurated the first silver coinage (though it seems he could not have, since no Aeginetan issues can be dated earlier than the mid-sixth century), are dumpy pieces with a turtle, clearly the badge of Aegina, on the obverse and a simple punch of crossed lines on the reverse. At nearby Athens, where coinage began about the same time, a variety of obverse designs was at first employed: animals (for example, horse, bull's head, beetle) or inanimate objects (amphora, wheel, triskeles and so on), which are thought to be the personal badges of individuals responsible for the issues. Again, just a simple punch was used for the reverse. At Corinth the first coins were much flatter, and the obverse design, depicting the winged horse Pegasus, was cut in lower relief. Here the punch on the reverse was formed into a swastika shape. Another difference between the coins is that each city-state used a different weight standard.

Other early producers of silver coinage in Greece included the cities of Chalcis, Eretria and Carystus in the island of Euboea, which used the same weight standard as Athens, with a stater of 17.2 g, but divided this into thirds, rather than quarters. The islands of the Cyclades, on the other hand, adopted the Aeginetan standard, with a two-drachma stater of 12.2 g, for their coinages.

Meanwhile, to the north of Greece, coinage also spread to the cities of the peninsula of Chalcidice in Macedonia, where the descendants of

7 *Early silver coins from Thrace and Macedonia:* (a) *Thasos, satyr and nymph;* (b) *Abdera, griffin facing left − note the ancient cut to test the coin's silver;* (c) *Teos, griffin facing right;* (d) 'Getas king of the Edoni' (inscribed on the reverse); (e) *Derrones;* (f) *Ichnai.*

Greek settlers adopted for their new coinages the weight standard used in their Euboean homeland. Further east coinage was also produced in Thrace. Major early producers here included the island of Thasos and the city of Abdera. Abdera was founded in 546 by Greek colonists from Teos, fleeing from the Persian advance through Asia Minor. The two cities both used a griffin design for their silver coins, but whereas in Teos the griffin always faced right, in Abdera it faced left.

In these northern areas coinage was also produced by the neighbours of the Greek settlers. Inland various tribes of semi-Greek or non-Greek peoples, usually referred to as Thraco-Macedonians, and often identified

only by the inscriptions on their coins – Ichnai, Edoni, Derrones, Bisalti and so on – began issuing silver coins towards the end of the sixth century and continued to flourish in the early fifth century. In style these are not unlike other early coins, with designs on one side and mostly simple punches or geometric patterns on the other, but they stand out because of their frequent use of large denominations of four-, eight- and even twelve-drachma pieces. Among their coin designs we find particularly types relating to the cult of Dionysus (nymphs with satyrs or centaurs) and 'rustic-looking' designs (huntsmen, herdsmen, ox-carts). These tribes were located in a region rich in silver mineral deposits, hence their production of large module coins, which according to hoard evidence travelled to the east in sizeable quantities, through trade or other means.

One of the most interesting areas of coin production in the later sixth century was the part of southern Italy earlier colonised by Achaean Greeks from the Peloponnese which came to be known as Magna Graecia ('Great Greece'). Its main cities were Metapontum, Sybaris, Croton and

8 *Silver coins of South Italy and Sicily, late 6th century* BC (a–c *have incuse reverses):* (a) *Sybaris, bull;* (b) *Metapontum, ear of barley;* (c) *Poseidonia, Poseidon with trident;* (d) *Velia, lion forepart;* (e) *Zancle, dolphin in Zancle's sickle-shaped harbour;* (f) *Selinus, wild parsley leaf.*

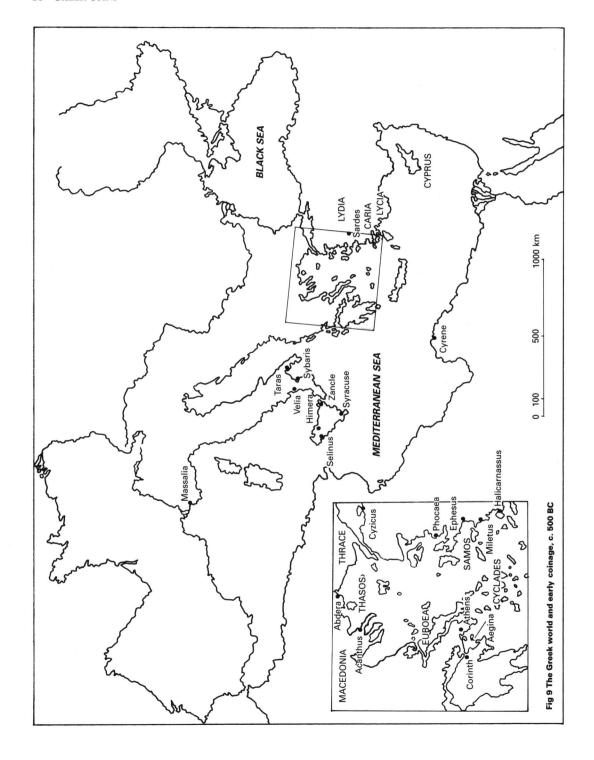

**Fig 9 The Greek world and early coinage, c. 500 BC**

BLACK SEA

LYDIA

Sardes

CARIA

LYCIA

CYPRUS

1000 km

500

Cyrene

MEDITERRANEAN SEA

100

0

Taras

Velia

Himera

Sybaris

Zancle

Syracuse

Selinus

Massalia

MACEDONIA

THRACE

Abdera

Acanthus

THASOS

Cyzicus

Phocaea

Ephesus

Halicarnassus

SAMOS

Miletus

EUBOEA

Athens

CYCLADES

Aegina

Corinth

Caulonia on the east coast and Poseidonia on the west. These cities all began producing silver coins in the second half of the sixth century, to the same 'Achaean' weight standard and with the same unusual technique, involving a single design reproduced in relief on the obverse and incuse on the reverse. So unusual and original is the style of manufacture that its invention has been ascribed (unfortunately without any evidence) to the famous scholar Pythagoras, who moved to Croton from Asia Minor in 530. The unique style at least suggests that this group of western Greeks developed their technique of manufacture independently, even if they copied the idea of coinage from other Greeks. Exactly when these 'incuse' coinages began is uncertain, but it is assumed that the substantial issues of Sybaris (and stylistically similar issues of the other cities) predate the destruction of that city by its rival Croton in 510.

The Achaean colonies were not the only early coin producers in this region. Other Greek cities in southern Italy issuing coins before 500 included Velia on the west coast, founded by Phocaean refugees in 540, and Taras on the east coast, Sparta's only colony. Velia's first coins, with a lion-forepart obverse design and punch-marked reverse, resemble very closely in style and fabric early electrum and silver coins of Asia Minor. The first coins of Taras, on the other hand, copied the 'incuse' technique of their Achaean neighbours. This technique was also used briefly towards the end of the sixth century for the coinage of one of the Greek cities in Sicily, Zancle (later renamed Messana), though most of Zancle's early coinage belonged to the more usual early Greek tradition, with a design on the obverse and a punch (or different design) on the reverse. Other cities in Sicily issuing substantial coinages before 500 included Naxos, Himera and Selinus.

Before we leave the sixth century mention should be made of the most eastern of the early coin producers, the island of Cyprus, and Cyrenaica on the coast of North Africa (in modern Libya). In the later sixth century both these regions had been incorporated into the Persian Empire, and some of the Cypriot cities were dominated by their Phoenician, rather than their Greek, populations, but they issued coins which are wholly 'Greek' in character. Recently analysed hoard evidence suggests that Cyprus may have had as many as ten minting cities active before the end of the sixth century, some producing coins of a quite 'advanced' style

9 Opposite *The Greek world and early coinage,* c. 500 BC.

10 *Silver coins of Cyprus and Cyrene, late 6th century:* **(a)** *double siglos, possibly minted at Paphos, depicting a bull and the head of an eagle;* **(b)** *tetradrachm from Cyrene with a silphium plant on the obverse.*

with designs on both sides. Cyrenaica, which had been colonised by Greeks since the seventh century, also enjoyed an impressive output of silver coinage before 500, with designs including the area's most famous product, the silphium plant, which was renowned for its healing qualities: '. . . Battus founded Cyrene, coming from Thera, the island near Crete. In his honour the Libyans dedicated to him the fairest of their plants, the silphium, and struck it upon their coinage' (Aristophanes, *Plutus* 924–5).

# CHAPTER 3

# The Fifth Century

T he most famous century of Greek history opened with the
threat of invasion from Persia and closed with the defeat of
Athens by her great rival Sparta at the end of the Peloponnesian
War. In between Athens had created an empire and built the temples of
the Acropolis. It was a period of unparalleled cultural achievement by
the Greeks, notably in art, with the works of the great sculptors Pheidias
and Polycleitus; in literature, with the playwrights Aeschylus, Sopho-
cles, Euripides and Aristophanes, and the historians Herodotus and
Thucydides; and in philosophy, with Socrates. The term 'Classical'
(meaning the highest standard against which all others can be measured)
has been used in general to cover the whole of ancient Greek and Roman
civilisations, but in the narrower sense to describe the Greeks' high-
point period from *c*. 480–323 BC. It is against this background of
recognised high achievement that the coinage of the fifth-century Greeks
should be viewed.

## The Persian Wars

Conflict with Persia was the dominant theme of Greek history in the first
half of the fifth century. King Darius (521–485) had crossed to Europe
to conquer Thrace *c*. 512, but then returned east. He decided on a
punitive expedition against the Greeks following his suppression of the
Ionic revolt against Persian rule in Asia Minor (499–494), since the
Greek cities of Athens and Eretria had joined the rebels in burning down
the city of Sardes in 498. When Darius' Persian troops and their allies
advanced against the Greeks in 492 (the reconquest of Thrace and
submission of Macedonia) and 490 (the attack on Eretria and Athens
which culminated in the Battle of Marathon), the coins they were using
were the gold Darics (so called after the king) and silver sigloi. These

11 *Coins of the Persians: silver sigloi (a–d) depicting the Great King (four types): half-figure of king, king with bow, king with bow and spear, king with bow and dagger;* **(e)** *gold double Daric of Babylonia, period of Alexander the Great, copying the third Persian type (c).*

coins had replaced the earlier 'Croeseid' issues *c.* 510. Instead of the old 'Lydian' lion-and-bull design on the obverse they depict a figure of the Great King, who appears in four different poses in the course of the series, which continued through the fifth and fourth centuries. The reverse retained a simple unmarked punch, giving the coins an immobilised primitive appearance. By far the largest of these Persian issues, particularly in silver sigloi, seem to date from the early decades of the fifth century, suggesting that their production was linked with the European operations of Darius and his successor Xerxes.

By the time of the Persian Wars coinage was well established in Greece. The early Athenian coins with changing obverse designs had been replaced by a more identifiably civic coinage with fixed designs on both sides: Athena on the obverse and her owl on the reverse – designs which were to remain on the coinage of Athens for centuries to come. The early 'owls' (known as 'unwreathed' because Athena's helmet is not decorated with a laurel wreath), dating from the period *c.* 510–480, were produced in huge quantities, providing the context for the story of Thucydides and the Athenian fleet mentioned earlier (p. 12). The wreath of olive leaves was introduced to the helmet of Athena *c.* 480–475, so it is tempting to link its introduction with a commemoration of the Greek victories against Xerxes' Persians.

The coinages of the other pioneering Greek minting cities also flourished in the early fifth century. The Aeginetans were great traders and their early 'turtles' are found abundantly in hoards wherever coinage reached. The influence of Aeginetan coinage is also clearly seen in the use of their weight standard by other coin producers, particularly in central

Greece, the Peloponnese and the Aegean islands. After the Persian Wars Aegina's commercial importance declined in the face of growing Athenian dominance. In the middle of the century, possibly following the Athenian conquest of Aegina in 457–456, the turtle on Aeginetan coins was replaced by a tortoise and coinage output was much reduced. Meanwhile at Corinth the appearance of the silver stater was changed towards the end of the sixth century by the addition of a head of Athena with Corinthian helmet as a reverse design to join the Pegasus on the obverse. These now became the permanent types on Corinthian silver staters. They were also used on the coins of Corinth's colonies in western Greece, two of which, Leucas and Ambracia, began minting coins early in the fifth century.

In central Greece the cities of Boeotia had formed a league under the leadership of Thebes. The unity of the league is declared by the use of a shared design of a shield on the obverse of all the coins of the league cities. Similar federations existed elsewhere in Greece, notably in Thessaly and Phocis. Everywhere coinage was exclusively in silver, though different denominations were favoured: the didrachm (two-drachma) in Boeotia, the drachm in Thessaly and the hemidrachm (half-drachma) and obol (sixth-drachma) in Phocis.

In the Peloponnese the southern areas dominated by Sparta produced no coins in the fifth century, but cities in the north-east were striking silver coinages, notably Sicyon and Argos, and the city of Elis produced regular issues of silver coinage which are assumed to be connected with

12 *Silver coins of Greece:* (a, b) *Athenian 'owls', 'unwreathed' and 'wreathed'; (c) 'tortoise' from Aegina;* (d) *Corinthian 'Pegasus' from the colony of Leucas.*

13 *Silver coins of Greek leagues of the 5th century:* **(a)** *didrachm of Thebes (Boeotian League);* **(b)** *drachm of Larissa in Thessaly;* **(c)** *hemidrachm of Phocis;* **(d)** *triobol of the Arcadian League, depicting a seated Zeus and head of Artemis.*

a     b     c     d

that city's control of the Olympic festival. Also, through the middle decades of the century, the Arcadian League produced a major coin series, largely issued in a single denomination, the triobol on the Aeginetan standard. This is recorded as being the standard daily rate of pay of an infantry soldier in 420 (Thucydides 5, 47), so it is tempting to see a mainly military purpose in this coinage.

## Sicily and Italy

While the Greeks were defeating the Persians in the Aegean, their western cousins in Sicily were overcoming their own oriental foes, the Carthaginians. Indeed, legend placed the Battle of Himera in 480, somewhat fancifully, on exactly the same day as the Battle of Salamis. At this date the important Greek cities of Sicily were ruled by tyrants: Theron at Acragas and his son-in-law Gelon and later Gelon's brother Hieron at Syracuse, Anaxilas at Rhegium and Zancle-Messana. These were Greek noblemen who ruled their cities like kings, spending lavishly on their courts and public buildings. They could be ruthless tyrants, frequently removing whole populations from city to city to establish or strengthen power bases. But they also aspired to be recognised as champions throughout the Greek world; they won and celebrated victories in the Olympic games and dedicated treasures at the Greek sanctuaries. Their coins provide another memorial. Though these usually record only the name of the city, and never of the ruler, it is possible to identify the issues produced in the period of the tyrannies.

The most clearly datable issues are the coins produced at Zancle following its seizure by refugees from Samos in 494. The Samians

14 *Bronze helmet discovered by a British tourist at Olympia in 1817. The inscription records it to be a votive offering by Hieron of Syracuse following a naval victory in 474 BC.*

15   replaced the earlier coin designs of Zancle with a lion-scalp type (imitating the coins of Samos) and a prow of a ship, with letters perhaps indicating the year. The Samians were themselves expelled *c.* 488 by Anaxilas of Rhegium, who then settled the city with Messenians from the Peloponnese and renamed it Messana. The Samian coinage of Zancle thus came to an abrupt end, but at least it provides a fixed point to help date other coinages from the region. Another issue that can certainly be dated to the period of the tyrants is a series of didrachms issued at Himera, struck to the same weight as coins of Acragas and with reverse type (a crab) borrowed from Acragantine coinage. These must surely date from the period (*c.* 483–472) when Himera was under the rule of Acragantine tyrants.

Under the tyrants Syracuse became the principal city and mint in Sicily. Gelon inaugurated a series of silver tetradrachms with a chariot crowned by Nike on the obverse (thought to be alluding to an Olympic victory won by Gelon in 488) and the head of the local sea-nymph Arethusa surrounded by dolphins on the reverse. An issue of these coins

15   in the larger denomination of decadrachms (ten drachmae) has been linked with a story recorded by the later Sicilian historian Diodorus: 'The Carthaginians [after the Battle of Himera] . . . also promised a gold crown to Damarete the wife of Gelon. . . . When she had been

15 *Silver coins of Sicily, 5th century:* (a) *issued by the Samians at Zancle;* (b) *the 'Demareteion' decadrachm of Syracuse;* (c) *tetradrachm of Naxos.*

presented by them with a crown of a hundred talents of gold, she struck a coin which was called a Demareteion after her. This contained ten Attic drachms . . .' (11, 26, 3). The problem with linking the extant decadrachms with this story is that they are made of silver, not gold, and hoard evidence suggests that they were struck not *c.* 479 but later, in the 460s, around the time of the fall of the Syracusan tyranny.

Before the middle of the century the tyrannies in Sicily had all been overthrown and the cities once more returned to self-rule. At Naxos an issue of silver tetradrachms was produced *c.* 460 for which only one pair of dies has so far been identified. The occasion is thought to be the return of the Naxian people to their city following earlier removal to Leontini by the tyrant Hieron of Syracuse. The coins have a bearded head of Dionysus on the obverse and a remarkable squatting Selinus on the reverse. Further south the Catanians marked their return home, following a similar exile, with an issue depicting the local river-god, as a man-headed bull, and a figure of Nike. Later they used a head of Apollo and chariot types, which had become common throughout Sicily, presumably through the influence of Syracuse. Among the issues of Catana from the later fifth century are examples of extraordinary fineness, sometimes signed by artists.

Most of the Greek cities of Sicily produced their finest coins in the later fifth century, and the names of artists appear on the coins of several

16 *Silver tetradrachm of Catana in Sicily, signed by the artist Herakleidas, c. 405 BC. (2 × actual size)*

mints, but the chief city of Syracuse produced the most remarkable coins of all. Output was concentrated on a long series of silver tetradrachms with the now standard types of a four-horse racing chariot, at first walking sedately, but later galloping, and the head of the nymph Arethusa. Details of the movement of the horses and the style of the Arethusa head exhibit great variety and imagination on the part of the die-engravers. The developing virtuosity reaches a peak with the issues of tetradrachms and decadrachms produced c. 415–400 by various artists whose names sometimes appear on the coins: Euainetos, Kimon, Eukleidas and others.

a       b       c

17 *The artists Euainetos and Kimon at Syracuse, Sicily: (a) Euainetos decadrachm; (b) Kimon tetradrachm with facing head of Arethusa; (c) Kimon decadrachm.*

18 *Coins of Acragas in Sicily:* (a) *silver decadrachm;* (b) *cone-shaped bronze coin with pellets denoting value* (=4 *unciae*) (2 × *actual size);* (c) *bronze 6-unciae coin.*

It is worth noting that these beautiful coins of Syracuse and the other Sicilian cities were produced during a period when the island was suffering invasions from Athens (415–413) and Carthage (409–405). The fall of Acragas to the Carthaginians in 406 provides a *terminus ante quem* (latest date possible) for the most remarkable coin produced by that city. This is the unsigned decadrachm apparently depicting the flying chariot of Helios the sun-god, a design which is thought to have been issued to celebrate the Olympic victory of Exainetos of Acragas in 412. The reverse of the coin has a composition showing two eagles standing triumphantly over their kill, a hare.

Other significant developments in the coinage of Sicily in the later fifth century included the introduction of the earliest Greek bronze coinages, at first cast into unusual shapes but later struck in the manner conventional for silver coins, and production of gold issues, which seem to have begun towards the end of the century at the time of the invasions. The Carthaginian colonies and the invading Carthaginian armies also began issuing their first coins at this time. Whether some were minted in Carthage or all in Sicily is uncertain, but they were clearly intended for circulation in the island and are thus referred to as 'Siculo-Punic'. The Carthaginians copied the local weight standards and coin designs, but

19 *Silver coins of Sicily and South Italy:* (a) *tetradrachm of the Carthaginians in Sicily, with inscriptions in Punic;* (b) *stater of Thurii in South Italy,* c. 415 BC.

they also produced issues with their own designs depicting horses, palm trees and inscriptions in Punic letters.

In Italy, as elsewhere, most fifth-century coinages were struck in silver. The 'incuse' style of manufacture used in the sixth century by the Achaean cities, such as Croton, Metapontum and Poseidonia, gradually gave way to conventional striking, with different designs in relief on both sides. Other Greek cities became prominent coin producers, including Cumae, the most northerly Greek colony, Neapolis, Terina, Taras and Thurii. Thurii was a Greek colony close to the site of Sybaris following a refoundation of the city assisted by Athens in 446. The influence of Athens is clear from the coin designs, which now bear a head of Athena on the obverse joining the old Sybarite bull. Bronze coins too were issued by Thurii and the importance of the city is evident from the later copying of its attractive Athena-head coin design at other cities, including Heraclea and Velia.

The westward expansion of coinage also continued in the fifth century, with the first issues produced in the area of Massalia in southern France c. 500. Massalia had been founded by Phocaean colonists and the influence of the coinage of their homeland in Asia Minor is clearly evident in the city's small silver coins. Similar issues have also appeared further west in the area of Emporium in northern Spain.

## Athens and the Peloponnesian War

Returning to the Aegean, the dominant power in the middle of the fifth century was Athens. After the Persian Wars the Delian League was formed by the Greek cities and islands of the Aegean as a defence against any repeated Persian aggression, but Athens assumed leadership of the league and in 454 removed its funds to the Athenian Acropolis. In time the league became an Athenian empire, and the contributions of the allies became tribute which could be used to enrich the city of Athens as well as for military needs: '. . . usually 600 talents came in annually to the city as tribute from the allies, apart from other income, and there were still on the Acropolis 6,000 talents of coined silver (the maximum had been 9,700 talents, from which expenditures had been made on the Propylaea of the Acropolis and on other buildings and for [the siege of] Potidea) . . .' (Thucydides, *Histories* 2, 13, 3–4). These are the words of Pericles, the Athenian leader, at the outbreak of the Peloponnesian War in 431 as reported by Thucydides. A talent of silver contained 6,000 drachmae, so 6,000 talents of coined silver would amount to the equivalent of nine million Athenian 'owl' tetradrachms. As Athenian dominance grew and the city's expenditure increased, more and more coinage was required and the 'owls' were produced in ever-increasing quantities (and in a broader range of denominations as the century progressed). At a date which is uncertain, but possibly in the 420s, the Athenians issued a decree forcing the use of Athenian coins, weights and measures on their allies. How effective this decree was is difficult to

**20** *Silver coins of Macedonia and Thrace, 5th century:* (**a**) *octadrachm of Alexander I of Macedon;* (**b**) *tetradrachm of Acanthus, lion and bull design;* (**c**) *tetradrachm of Mende, Dionysus on an ass;* (**d**) *tetradrachm of Abdera, griffin;* (**e**) *Aenus, Hermes/ goat.*

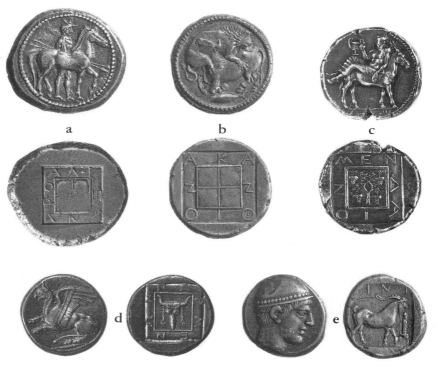

gauge. Some mints may have closed in the 420s, but others seem to have ceased minting earlier, around the middle of the century, and some apparently continued minting without a break. It is likely that the political and commercial dominance of Athens and her abundant coinage was already causing local coinages to cease with or without a decree.

Surviving inventories of valuables held in sanctuaries at Athens, Eleusis, Delphi, Delos and elsewhere provide glimpses of the currency in circulation. As a typical example a few extracts from Athens (*Accounts of the Treasurers of the Other Gods*) from 429/8 BC can be quoted: '5 hektai of Cyzicene gold. 105 staters of Daric gold. 5 hektai of Phocaean gold . . . 340 Aeginetan staters. 489 Chian silver drachmas. 26 Corinthian staters. Acanthian silver, 386 drachmas. . . .' (*IG* I³, 383, 15–32).

Coin hoards provide another, broadly similar, view. They confirm that in the mid- and late fifth century new mint cities had come to prominence in the Aegean area. In the north the 'tribal' coinages had ceased; in mid-century Alexander I of Macedon was a major coin producer, and the cities of Acanthus and Mende in Macedonia and Abdera and Aenus in Thrace were all producing silver coins. In the east Aegean most cities and islands produced only small-denomination

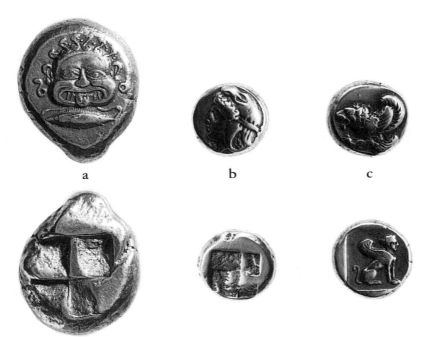

a     b     c

21 *Electrum coins of Asia Minor, 5th to 4th centuries (2 × actual size):* (a) *Cyzicus stater with Gorgon head;* (b) *Phocaea, sixth-stater, head with Phrygian cap;* (c) *Lesbos, sixth-stater, winged lion/ sphinx.*

silver, but Chios and Samos issued larger silver coins, and, as noted in the above inventory, Cyzicus and Phocaea issued 'gold' coinages (in reality electrum). Cyzicus issued electrum staters and fractions, in the old 'dumpy' style of the early electrum, through the fifth and fourth centuries, and Phocaea issued sixth-stater pieces, which for a time in the early fourth century were produced in alternate years with the city of Mytilene in Lesbos.

The Peloponnesian War (431–404) between Athens and Sparta involved most of the city-states in Greece and the Aegean. Its most visible impact on the coinage of Athens was seen after the Spartan occupation of Decelea in Attica in 413 caused the closure of the silver mines of Laurium. Without their silver mines, and with their former allies deserting them and no longer paying tribute, the Athenians could no longer mint silver coins. As an emergency measure the hard-pressed Athenians produced bronze coins plated with silver and they made gold coins from metal stored in the temples on the Acropolis. Seven statues of Victory were melted down in an operation which yielded 84,000 gold staters of coinage, some examples of which survive today.

The Spartans still did not use coinage, but their Peloponnesian allies did, and it is interesting that Sicyon emerged at this time as the principal mint on the Peloponnese, completely eclipsing Corinth. The silver staters of Sicyon, struck to the Aeginetan standard, may have been established as the agreed 'major' currency, with many other cities providing their own small-denomination pieces.

In the later years of the Peloponnesian War the Persians re-emerged as a force in the politics of the Aegean area. They formed an alliance with Sparta, by which they would agree to finance the Peloponnesian fleet in the eastern Aegean in return for Spartan recognition of their claims over the Greek cities of Asia Minor. With Persian support the Spartans eventually won the war and it is likely that an increase in production of Persian sigloi and, especially, gold Darics can be dated to this period and its aftermath, when increasing numbers of Greek mercenaries were employed in Persian armies. The end of the Athenian empire was also marked by a revival of coinage production in many of the former subject cities around the Aegean.

In the course of the fifth century coinage had also spread to new areas in the eastern Mediterranean: the island of Crete, Pamphylia and Cilicia

III,

21

22

**22** *Silver stater of Sicyon (1.5 × actual size), depicting the chimaera and a dove.*

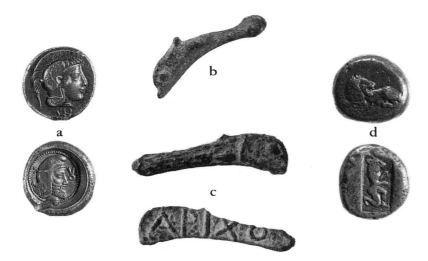

23 *Coins of Asia Minor and the Black Sea region:* (a) *silver stater of Lycia, portraying the dynast Kharai on the reverse;* (b, c) *bronze dolphins of Olbia, one with the name of an official;* (d) *silver stater from Colchis, with designs of a lion and a bull-headed figure (the Minotaur?).*

in southern Turkey, and the cities of the Phoenician coast, including Tyre and Sidon. An interesting development, significant for the future of coinage, was the introduction of portraiture. The earliest example is a bearded head of the great Athenian statesman Themistocles which appears on a small silver fraction issued by the city of Magnesia in Asia Minor, which he governed on behalf of King Artaxerxes of Persia *c.* 460, following his exile from Athens. The rulers of Lycia also began to be portrayed on their coins later in the fifth century.

Another region where coinage spread in the fifth century was the Black Sea. From Asia Minor it extended eastwards along the sea's southern shores to the Greek cities of Sinope and Trapezus. On the sea's western shores the Greek colonies of Apollonia Pontica, Mesembria and Istrus began striking coins in the late fifth century, as also did the city of Panticapaeum in the north. Olbia, also in the north, began with cast bronze 'coins' in the shape of dolphins, before striking more conventional coins in the fourth century. Finally, from the Greek settlements in Colchis on the Black Sea's eastern shore, comes a 'dumpy' silver coin with a primitive appearance, perhaps dating from *c.* 400.

# CHAPTER 4

# The Fourth Century

I n 400 BC an army of 10,000 Greek mercenaries was retreating through Asia towards Greece, having defeated a Persian army in Babylonia. The adventure of the 10,000, chronicled by one of their number, the historian Xenophon, was a forerunner of a much greater enterprise, the conquest of the Persian Empire by Alexander the Great later in the fourth century. In the early fourth century Greece was still dominated by the city-states, first Sparta, then Thebes and the Boeotian League, but after Philip II became king of Macedonia in 359 he first enlarged the Macedonian kingdom and later became undisputed leader of the Greeks, laying the foundation for his son Alexander's conquests. And after Alexander the Greek world would be changed forever. What does the coinage show of these dramatic and far-reaching events?

## Greece and the Aegean

In the early and mid-fourth century the coinage produced around the Aegean was immensely varied and illustrates a society in which the dominant political unit was still the city-state, either individually or united in regional federations. In Greece production of 'tortoises' was revived at Aegina, and of 'owls' at Athens, and Corinth became a major coin producer again. Stylistic developments clearly separate these coins from fifth-century issues: letters and symbols, acting as control marks, were added to the traditional designs at Aegina and Corinth, and at Athens the head of the goddess was given an eye drawn in naturalistic profile, rather than in the 'archaic' frontal style used in the fifth century.

Stylistic or developmental changes can also be seen in other issues. The principal series produced by Thebes, dating from the period of that city's supremacy in the region, from the 370s to the 330s, had the usual Theban designs of a Boeotian shield on the obverse and an amphora on

24 *Silver coins of the Aegean region, 4th century:* (a) *Thebes, with name of magistrate in abbreviated form on the reverse;* b) *Chalcidian League;* (c–e) *facing heads at Amphipolis, Larissa and Clazomenae.*

the reverse, but the latter was now accompanied by a personal name in abbreviated form. Again this would have acted as a control mark, identifying the issue as belonging to a particular period and supervising official. These Theban coins are common in hoards from the Peloponnese as well as central Greece.

In Macedonia the most abundant coinage in the late fifth and early fourth centuries was that of the Chalcidian League, which issued silver tetradrachms and fractions. On the obverse was a head of Apollo and on the reverse a lyre, or, for the smallest denominations, a tripod, both standard attributes of Apollo. After 379 the tetradrachms also bore the name of an official. The many fourth-century coin hoards containing tetradrachms and tetrobols (each worth one-sixth of a tetradrachm) of the league illustrate the importance of these coins. It is also significant that Philip II of Macedonia later adopted the league's weight standard for his silver coinage and borrowed the obverse Apollo-head design for his own gold coins.

Many of the coinages produced in the Aegean area in this period are notable for their attractive designs. Facing heads had become something

24

25 Overleaf *Map of the Aegean region.*

**Fig 25 The Aegean region**

THRACE

Byzantium

aenus

Parium     Cyzicus

BITHYNIA

MYSIA

Mytilene     Pergamum

LYDIA

Myrina

Phocaea

Smyrna     Sardes

Clazomenae

SAMOS     Ephesus

R. Maeander

Miletus

CARIA

PAMPHYLIA

Aspendus

Halicarnassus

Side

LYCIA

RHODES

Antiphellus

0     50     100 km

of a fashion, perhaps inspired by some of the recent Syracusan master-pieces. At Amphipolis in Macedonia a new series of tetradrachms, struck to the same weight standard as the Chalcidian League coinage, began in the late fifth century. These depict a three-quarter facing head of Apollo on the obverse and a torch within a framed square on the reverse. A similar head, but of a female city-deity closely similar to Kimon's facing Arethusa at Syracuse, was used for the obverse of the silver coins of Larissa in Thessaly in the fourth century. Other cities adopting facing-head designs in this period included Aenus in Thrace, Rhodes and Clazomenae in Asia Minor, where a series of beautiful gold staters and silver tetradrachms was produced, depicting a facing head of Apollo on the obverse and a swan on the reverse. One of the dies for this coinage was signed by an artist called Theodotos.

Some of the most striking coins from this period were produced in the Peloponnese. In a region where most cities (with the notable exceptions of Elis and Sicyon) had previously concentrated on issues of small-denomination coins, we suddenly find in the 360s production of silver didrachm-staters. At each city a fine head of a deity was used as the obverse type: Zeus on the coins of the Arcadian League, Hera at Argos, Artemis at Stymphalus and Demeter at Pheneus. Again the inspiration provided by earlier Syracusan coin designs is apparent. The reverse designs, usually figures of gods, are equally fine. It is believed that this sudden outburst of 'prestige' coinage production must have been occasioned by the release from Spartan oppression following the victory of the Boeotian League over the Spartans in the Battle of Leuctra in 371 BC. Inter-city rivalry may also have played its part.

26 *Silver staters of the Peloponnese:* (a) *Arcadian League, Zeus/Pan seated;* (b) *Argos, Hera/dolphins;* (c) *Stymphalus, Artemis/ Heracles striking with club;* (d) *Pheneus, Demeter/ Hermes with the child Arcas.*

a     b     c     d

An event in fourth-century Greek history which can clearly be seen reflected in the coinage is the Third Sacred War, 356–346. Following their seizure of Delphi in 356, the Phocians employed a mercenary army in their defence. The silver coins produced by the Phocians to pay their mercenaries depict a head of Apollo, in recognition of their control of Apollo's sanctuary, and, as we have seen, one of the main sources of metal for the Phocians' coinage was the temple treasures. On their bronze coins appear the names of two of their generals, Onymarchus and Phalaecus: 'After Onymarchus had been chosen as general in sole command, he prepared a large supply of weapons from the bronze and the iron, and struck coinage from the silver and the gold . . .' (Diodorus Siculus 16, 33, 2).

The Phocians were finally forced to give up Delphi in 346 and to repay the plundered treasury at the rate of sixty talents a year (360,000 drachms). Ten years later the Amphictionic Council, which administered the Delphic sanctuary, decided to produce a series of coinage in its own name, minted from existing stocks of miscellaneous coinage. Some of the accounts of the treasurers have survived and these have provided crucial evidence for reconstructing from this example ancient Greek minting activity. The coins produced by the Amphictions, in three denominations of silver, have a head of Demeter on the obverse, and on the reverse of the stater and drachm is a figure of Apollo seated on his sacred stone, the omphalos.

27

27 *Coins of Phocis:*
(a) *bronze coin in the name of Onymarchus;* (b) *silver stater of the Amphictionic Council.*

Another coinage of this period from central Greece that is worthy of special mention was issued by the Locrians of Opus. The obverse design copied the Arethusa head on Syracusan coinage by the artist Euainetos, and on the reverse was a figure of the local hero Ajax, leader of the Locrians in the Trojan War. These coins were issued in staters and

28

**28** *Silver stater of the Opuntian Locrians (compare the obverse head with fig. 17a). (2 × actual size)*

smaller denominations for a few decades in the mid-fourth century, and they were sufficiently numerous to have circulated quite widely in central Greece, but they were an isolated series: no coins of comparable importance or beauty were ever again issued by the Opuntian Locrians.

## The west

For the western Greeks the fourth century was a troubled period and the vicissitudes of the different colonies can be seen in the pattern of coinage output.

At the start of the fourth century much of Sicily was under the control of the Carthaginians, but in the east Syracuse retained its independence under the tyrant Dionysius I (405–367). These two powers were now the only significant coin producers. The Carthaginians had two principal mints on the island, 'Ziz' (probably Panormus) and, after *c.* 350, 'Rash Melkarth' (possibly Selinus). These mints issued copies of Syracusan tetradrachms, with the head of Arethusa now representing the Carthaginian goddess Tanit. Other Siculo-Punic issues cannot be attributed to particular mints, having Punic inscriptions translating as 'Carthage', or the explicitly military references 'camp' or 'people of the camp'. These include some interesting and attractive designs dominated by the recurring Carthaginian emblems of palm trees and horses. The horse's head reminds us of the foundation legend of Carthage recorded by Virgil: '. . . the spot where first the Phoenicians, tossed by waves and whirlwind, dug up the token which queenly Juno had pointed out, a head of the spirited horse; for thus was the race to be famous in war and rich in substance through the ages' (*Aeneid* 1, 442–5).

a   b   c

29 *Coins of Sicily, 4th century:* (a, b) *Siculo-Punic silver tetradrachms,* (a) *the head of Tanit closely copying Euainetos' Arethusa from Syracuse (compare fig. 17a);* (c) *gold 100-litra coin of Syracuse signed by Euainetos.*

Perhaps the most attractive Siculo-Punic coin is a mid-fourth-century tetradrachm depicting the head of a goddess on the obverse with oriental headgear (sometimes mistakenly identified as Queen Dido) and a lion and palm tree on the reverse. Meanwhile, in the later fourth century, a mint was also opened in Carthage itself, producing gold staters and fractions with types of a Tanit head and standing horse.

The coinage of Dionysius I of Syracuse also contains some memorable pieces. Production of silver tetradrachms ceased *c*. 400, but the decadrachms signed by Euainetos continued, and these, together with new denominations in gold, also sometimes signed by Euainetos and Kimon, were no doubt produced mainly for the payment of the mercenaries Dionysius needed for his long struggle against the Carthaginians. The reverse design on the gold 100-litra piece (worth two decadrachms) depicts Heracles wrestling with the Nemean lion, perhaps symbolising Dionysius' struggle against his barbarian enemy.

When, in 344, the mercenary leader Timoleon arrived in Sicily from Corinth to help the Syracusans, there was very little Greek coinage left in circulation on the island. This vacuum was soon filled by Corinthian coinage, which became the standard currency in Greek Sicily for several decades. Most of the 'Pegasi' came from Corinth itself, though some were supplied by the Corinthian colonies in north-western Greece and even by local production at Syracuse and briefly at Leontini. Bronze coins were also produced at Syracuse with Corinthian-inspired designs, celebrating Timoleon's liberation of the Sicilian Greeks. These bronze issues also include depictions of Zeus Eleutherios ('the liberator').

30 *Coins of Syracuse in Sicily from the time of Timoleon:* (a) *locally minted Corinthian 'Pegasus';* (b) *bronze coin depicting Zeus Eleutherios ('liberator').*

The drastic curtailment of Greek mints in Sicily was not repeated in southern Italy, though here also the Greeks were struggling against enemies, mostly native tribes of the interior, and production ceased at some of the old mint cities. The city of Neapolis became the major mint in the Campanian region, with its silver staters depicting the head of the siren Parthenope on the obverse and the man-headed bull Achelous, father of the sirens, crowned by Nike flying above, on the reverse. Bronze coinage was also produced in large quantities at Neapolis from the mid-fourth century.

31 *Coins of South Italy, 4th century:* (a) *Neapolis;* (b) *Taras, horseman/Taras on dolphin;* (c) *Thurii, Athena/bull;* (d) *Heraclea;* (e) *Taras, gold stater (see also pl. V);* (f) *South Italian silver coin of Alexander of Epirus.*

Other prominent mint cities were Velia, further down the west coast, and, on the south coast, Taras, Thurii, Heraclea and Metapontum. Silver was still the most important metal for coinage, and some brilliant coin designs continued to be produced, with artists' signatures again appearing. The city of Heraclea had been founded jointly by Thurii and Taras in 433; its choice of coin designs (Athena on the obverse and Heracles on the reverse) was therefore natural. The Heracles and Nemean lion type may have been selected simply for design reasons, but considering the difficulties the Greek cities of this region were having with the native tribes it was a particularly apt scene, which could be seen as symbolic of the Greeks' struggle against hostility in their environment (cf. Dionysius in Sicily). In this region there was also occasional production of larger-denomination silver and gold coins, probably required for the hiring of mercenary armies, which were frequently invited over from Greece to aid the cities in their defence. Taras, in particular, sought help from its mother city Sparta, and one of its superb gold coins has a design apparently symbolising this action, depicting a young boy raising his arms in appeal to the seated god Poseidon. One of the mercenary leaders, Alexander of Epirus, who was in Italy 334–330, struck his own coinage at Taras and elsewhere with designs similar to those of the Syracusan bronzes after Timoleon.

## The east

East of the Aegean area coinage production continued to increase and spread in the fourth century. In Asia Minor output of Persian silver sigloi seems to have declined, but there was increased production of silver issues by local dynasts or Persian satraps (provincial governors). Of particular interest are the coinages of well-known historical figures, such as Maussolus, dynast of Caria 377–353, whose magnificent colonnaded tomb has given the word 'mausoleum' to the English language, or the

a                                b

32 *Silver staters of Asia Minor:* (a) *Maussolus, dynast of Caria, Apollo/ Zeus;* (b) *the satrap Pharnabazus at Cyzicus (note the tunny fish, symbol of the city, below the warship).*

satrap Pharnabazus of Dascylium (413–370), whose portrait appears on silver coins minted at Cyzicus. It has been suggested that these coins, which depict the prow of a war galley on the reverse, were minted in 396 in connection with the assistance given by Pharnabazus to the Athenian admiral Conon while he was besieged by the Spartans at Caunus in Caria. Cyzicus produced a regular output of silver coinage for much of the fourth century, but at the same time continued to strike its old-fashioned-looking electrum coinage, which from the evidence of hoards and inscriptions had a wide circulation as a 'gold' trade coinage in the Black Sea region and Greece.

Further east there was much increased production of local coinage in the fourth century, especially in silver. The cities of Cilicia produced varied and interesting issues, some in their own name, others signed by Persian satraps. It is likely that much of this coinage was produced in connection with military operations led by the satraps: Tiribazus (386–360) against Cyprus, and Pharnabazus and Datames against Egypt (379–363). Another interesting feature of the Cilician coinages is their

**33** *Silver coins (double sigloi) of Cilicia, 4th century (2 × actual size):* **(a)** *the satrap Pharnabazus at Tarsus;* **(b)** *the city of Mallus.*

a                  b

copying of designs which derive from Greek coins from as far away as Sicily and South Italy. Kimon's facing Arethusa head from Syracuse makes yet another appearance (on the satrapal coinage of Tarsus, which also adopted the helmeted Athena head of Athens but added a beard), a standing Heracles from Heraclea in South Italy was copied at Issus, and at Mallus the Heracles and Nemean lion design familiar from Heraclean coinage was coupled with a demonstrably Achaemenid image of the running royal archer.

In Phoenicia, where there was also significant expansion of coinage in the fourth century, the coin designs were more consistently oriental. The kings of Sidon overtly pronounced their allegiance to the Achaemenids with coin designs depicting a crowned figure presumed to be the Persian Great King in various scenes which are often repeated in Achaemenid royal seals.

Cyprus continued to be a major coin producer, with gold and bronze issues now added to the well-established and prolific silver coinage of the various cities. New areas of coin production within the Persian Empire included Egypt and Palestine. In Egypt imitation Athenian 'owls' were now minted locally, presumably to supplement the dwindling stocks of fifth-century Athenian coinage on which Egypt had hitherto mainly relied. Production of Egyptian 'owls' continued until the time of King Artaxerxes III (358–337), whose name appears on some examples in Egyptian Demotic script. Owls also appear in Palestine among the designs used in a silver coinage issued in various denominations, but mostly small fractions, usually referred to as 'Philisto-Arabian'. The places of origin of these coins are uncertain, but many are thought to be from Gaza; one group which is inscribed 'Judaea' in Aramaic letters may be from Jerusalem, and is usually identified as the earliest Jewish coinage.

a

b

34 *Silver coins of Egypt and Judaea, 4th century:* (a) *Egyptian imitation Athenian 'owl' in the name of Artaxerxes Pharaoh;* (b) *Judaean silver drachm with a helmeted male head and deity seated on a winged wheel.*

## Philip and Alexander

In the later fourth century the pattern of coinage circulation in Greece gradually changed as local coinages were supplanted by Macedonian regal issues, first of Philip II (359–336) and later of his son Alexander III (336–323), known as Alexander the Great. This process seems to have begun soon after Philip II acquired the rich silver and gold mines of the Mount Pangaeus area in 357–356: 'He then went to the city of Krenides, expanded its population greatly and changed its name to Philippi after himself; and he increased the output of the small and insignificant gold mines in the area so much by his improvements that they were able to bring him a revenue of more than a thousand talents' (Diodorus Siculus 16, 8, 6).

This increased wealth enabled Philip to expand the Macedonian kingdom, and use of his gold and silver coins and those of his successor Alexander, produced in ever-increasing quantities, gradually spread throughout Greece. It is difficult to date precisely the end of civic coinages. The Chalcidian League's coinage ceased abruptly when Philip destroyed the league with its capital Olynthus in 348, and the coinage of the Boeotian Confederacy came to a similar end when Thebes was destroyed by Alexander in 335. For most issues the end was probably not so dramatic – the output of drachms at Larissa, for instance, seems to have continued until *c.* 320 – but coin hoards buried in the last decades of the fourth century show clearly and consistently that by the end of the century Macedonian regal issues provided the dominant large-denomination coinage throughout Greece, Macedonia, Thrace and the Aegean coastlands of Asia Minor, with local production largely confined to issues of silver fractions and bronze.

35 *Coins of Philip II of Macedon:* (a) *gold stater;* (b) *silver stater depicting Philip on horseback.*

According to Plutarch (*Alexander* 4, 5), Philip II 'had the victories of his chariots at Olympia stamped upon his coins'. His gold coins depict a two-horse racing chariot on the reverse and a head of Apollo on the obverse. On his silver coins the head of Zeus was used on the obverse with a horseman on the reverse. There are two versions of the horseman: on one a racing jockey holds a palm branch; on the other Philip himself, wearing the Macedonian flat cap (kausia), gives a victory salute. The coinage of Philip, which also included gold and silver fractions and bronze issues, was produced in parallel at two separate mints, presumed to be Amphipolis and Pella.

After Philip's death, production of his coinage, at least in gold, continued for a time under Alexander, and his coin types were revived under Philip III Arrhidaeus (323–317) and again later, alongside posthumous issues of Alexander's own coinage, so firmly established had the reputation and acceptability of the Macedonian coinage become. Alexander's own coin types were the head of Heracles and a seated Zeus on the silver, and a head of Athena and a standing Nike (Victory) on the gold. These were the images chosen to decorate the coinage with which Alexander set out to conquer the Persian Empire, carrying out the mission his father had already planned and been elected to lead by the Hellenic League meeting at Corinth. Heracles was the legendary ancestor of the Macedonian royal house, and he appeared frequently on its coinage. Zeus and Athena were appropriate deities for Alexander to be associated with in his position as new leader of the Hellenic League.

a       b       c

36 *Coins of Alexander the Great, minted in Macedonia during his lifetime and later:* (a) *silver tetradrachm and* (c) *gold stater of the main Macedonian mint (Amphipolis?), lifetime;* (b) *silver 'posthumous' Alexander tetradrachm attributed to the mint of Amphipolis,* c. 294–290 BC.

Victory no doubt looks forward to the forthcoming war against Persia, but this specific Victory figure carries a ship's mast (stylis), emblematic of war at sea and perhaps recalling the great naval victory of the Greeks over the Persians at Salamis in 480.

Alexander at first followed his father's system of minting coins to two weight standards: Attic for the gold coinage, that of the Chalcidian League for the silver; but soon he abandoned the latter in favour of the Attic standard for the silver also. Having the same weight as the legendary Athenian 'owls', the silver tetradrachms of Alexander, minted in enormous quantities as his empire expanded, soon became as ubiquitous as the old 'owls' had been.

As Alexander and his army marched eastwards new mints were required to provide cash to pay his troops and the expenses of his campaigning and to convert the booty of his conquests into Macedonian imperial coinage. Some of the cities had already been striking coins while under Persian control – for example, Tarsus in Cilicia, Salamis in Cyprus and Phoenician cities, such as Aradus and Sidon. But other mints were completely new, such as Ake in Phoenicia, Damascus in Syria and further east the major mint he set up in Babylon.

In addition to the major imperial issues in gold and silver, other coinages were also produced under Alexander. In Egypt he minted a rare

37 *Silver coins of Alexander the Great minted in the east:* (a) *double siglos from Tarsus in Cilicia;* (b, c) *'Porus medallions':* (b) *the decadrachm showing Alexander attacking a war elephant on one side and holding a thunderbolt on the other side;* (c) *the tetradrachm depicting an Indian bowman and an Indian elephant.*

a             b             c

series of bronze coins with his own portrait, possibly at the time of his visit in 332. In some areas he sanctioned the production of 'local' issues alongside his own. In Cilicia, for instance, the earlier satrapal series, struck to the Persian weight standard and with the local god Baal of Tarsus on the reverse, survived under Alexander's governor Balakros, though a new obverse design was introduced, depicting a facing head of Athena. Similar eastern 'local' issues included the 'lion staters' of Babylonia and the gold double Darics of Mesopotamia, imitating the earlier Persian Darics of Asia Minor. Finally the most striking of all Alexander's coins are the so-called 'Porus medallions' of ten drachmae (or five shekels), depicting Alexander on Bucephalus attacking a mounted war elephant; and associated tetradrachms, depicting an Indian bow-man, a war chariot and war elephants. These rare coins, minted somewhere in the east towards the end of his reign, provide eloquent illustrations of Alexander's eastern adventure.

## The diadochi

Upon Alexander's early death in 323 at the age of thirty-two his empire passed into the hands of his generals, known as the diadochi ('successors'), who for a time governed on behalf of Alexander's joint heirs, his half-brother Philip III and his infant son (born posthumously) Alexander IV. Coinage with the types of Alexander the Great continued to be issued, in the name of either Alexander (presumably standing for Alexander IV) or Philip (Philip III). There was also a revival of the gold and silver coinage with types of Philip II at the Macedonian mints of Pella and Amphipolis, probably because of the popularity of these coins in the Balkans, and in the far east the 'lion staters' of Babylonia continued, as well as the gold double Darics and more imitation 'owls', some in the name of the satrap Mazaces.

By 306 both Philip III and Alexander IV were dead and the generals had divided the empire between themselves: Ptolemy taking Egypt, Cassander Macedonia and Greece, Lysimachus Thrace, Antigonus Monophthalmus ('One-eyed') western Asia Minor and Seleucus the eastern provinces. The coinage of Alexander the Great continued to be issued, because of its popularity and acceptability, and when it was replaced by new designs these included portraits of the now deified

38  *Coins of Ptolemy I of
Egypt with his portrait:*
(a) *gold stater;* (b) *silver
tetradrachm.*

Alexander, because the diadochi were all anxious to emphasise their
association with the conqueror. Thus, in *c.* 320 Ptolemy introduced a
new coinage in Egypt with a portrait of Alexander wearing an elephant-
scalp headdress; the reverse retained Alexander's name and seated Zeus
design. This new coinage was probably introduced following Ptolemy's
hijacking in 321 of Alexander's corpse, *en route* from Babylon to
Macedonia, which he had buried amid great ceremony in Alexandria.

However, the diadochi also wished to create their own kingdoms and
found dynasties, and so we see on some of their coins the gradual
assertion of monarchical authority: the introduction of personal or
dynastic coin types, use of the title basileus (king) and ultimately the
adoption of personal portraiture. Ptolemy's own name started appearing
on his coins between 315 and 310, in 305 he adopted the title king and
finally, around the end of the century, his own gruesomely realistic
portrait appears. On his gold coinage the portrait, which has Ptolemy          38
diademed and wearing the aegis, is accompanied by a reverse design
depicting the deified Alexander holding a thunderbolt and riding in a
chariot drawn by elephants; on the silver the reverse has an eagle and          38
thunderbolt design which had earlier been used as a subsidiary design
element in Ptolemy's coinage and was to become the recurring symbol of
his dynasty. These coins clearly illustrate Ptolemy's intention to promote a personal cult through association with Zeus and the deified
Alexander.

# CHAPTER 5

# The Third Century

T he third century began with the surviving diadochi still
fighting to establish or defend their separate power bases in the
eastern Mediterranean. Three great kingdoms eventually emerged: Macedonia, ruled by the Antigonid house, descended from Antigonus the One-eyed and his son Demetrius I; Egypt, ruled by the
Ptolemies; and Syria and much of Asia Minor, ruled by the descendants
of Seleucus. Some smaller independent kingdoms also emerged, including Pergamum, Bithynia and Pontus in Asia Minor, and in the mid-
third century the eastern territories of the Seleucid empire seceded to
form the independent kingdoms of Parthia and Bactria. Meanwhile
further west a new power – Rome – was emerging to a position of
prominence in central Italy. Rome would eventually become the dominant power throughout the Mediterranean, but in the third century the
impact on the Greek world of Rome's expansion was felt only by the
Greek colonies in Italy and Sicily and by the Carthaginians.

## The coinage of Alexander and the diadochi

The coinage of Alexander was the most common and widespread ancient
currency at the beginning of the third century. In addition to the huge
output from Alexander's lifetime, numerous issues of Alexander-type
coinage continued to be produced after his death in 323; indeed, the
number of mints issuing Alexander coins increased following this date,
and so did their geographical spread, with new (posthumous) Alexander
mints in Greece, Thrace, Mesopotamia and Persia. But regal coinages in
the names of the successors were also being produced in the new
kingdoms. In Egypt Ptolemy had been the first to cease production of
Alexander coins, and by the early third century changes in the weight
standards of his coinage meant that Egypt effectively became a closed

**39** *Silver coins of Alexander's successors: Alexander's head appears on tetradrachms of* (a) *Seleucus I (the reverse shows Nike crowning a trophy) and* (b) *Lysimachus of Thrace (reverse, seated Athena);* (c) *tetradrachm of Demetrius I of Macedon with the king's portrait (reverse, seated Poseidon).*

currency zone where only Ptolemaic coinage could circulate. Elsewhere, though, the same (Attic) weight standard was generally employed for the new coinages, so they could circulate alongside Alexander coins and each other.

Fresh coin designs were introduced, but the influence of Alexander's coinage was always apparent. The new portrait heads clearly evolved from Alexander's Heracles head. Thus Seleucus issued coins with a portrait, presumed to be Alexander as Dionysus, conqueror of the east, in a panther-skin helmet, and the coins of Lysimachus depict another portrait, unquestionably of Alexander this time, with the ram's horn of Zeus Ammon, the god whom Alexander had claimed as his father. Demetrius followed Ptolemy in using his own portrait on some coins, though again the portrait has divine attributes (the bull's horn of Poseidon), like Alexander's Heracles. For their reverse designs, the new coins also usually followed recent Macedonian tradition with figures of gods, standing, seated (the commonest form) or riding.

There are also coin designs from this period which allude to the wars of the diadochi: Demetrius issued coins early in the fourth century which clearly celebrate a naval victory, presumed to be his earlier defeat (306 BC) of Ptolemy's fleet off the coast of Cyprus. Many other coins without explicitly military designs were also associated with the wars. A rare issue of Athenian gold coinage with the usual types of the city can be linked to the period when Athens was under siege from Demetrius (296)

40 *Coins of the period of the diadochi:* (a) *Demetrius I of Macedon, silver tetradrachm alluding to a naval victory;* (b) *gold stater of Athens, period of Lachares;* (c) *bronze coin of Seleucus I minted at Apamea in Syria;* (d) *gold stater in the name of King Agathocles, Syracuse.*

and the tyrant Lachares was forced to use gold from the cult statue of Athena to pay his troops. This is one of only a few issues of Athenian coinage produced between the fourth and second centuries.

Bronze coinage was by now issued as regularly as silver, and all the diadochi produced substantial issues. It is, however, noticeable that royal portraits never seem to appear among the many designs used on the bronze coins of the diadochi. On the bronze coin of Seleucus illustrated, one side depicts a war elephant, the other a horse, perhaps Alexander's famous mount Bucephalus. The inscription identifies King Seleucus, as does the anchor, personal badge of Seleucus (and later the Seleucid dynasty) because of an anchor-shaped birthmark on his thigh.

In 281 the last two remaining diadochi, Lysimachus and Seleucus, were both killed, but the legacy of Alexander and his successors on Greek coinage remained. The dynasties established by Ptolemy, Seleucus and the Antigonids provided long series of kings, many of whose portraits appeared on the coins, following the tradition introduced by Ptolemy, Demetrius and Seleucus. Alexander's coinage continued to be issued posthumously, with new concentrations in the Black Sea region and in the cities of western Asia Minor, where it was now needed for paying protection money to invading Celtic tribes. The Alexander coinage was also imitated widely, and not just in the area of his former empire. In the west, for instance, Agathocles of Syracuse (317–289) issued a series of gold coins in the early third century with a head of Athena copying exactly the staters of Alexander. In addition, 'barbarous' copies of Alexander's coinage were made in Arabia and in Europe by Celtic and other tribes, particularly in the region to the north of Greece; further west, the Celtic tribes of the Danube and beyond showed a preference for the coinage of Philip II.

The coinage of Lysimachus had a lasting influence, too. By the time of his death it had become well established in the Black Sea region, and because of its popularity with the Celtic tribes in the Balkans posthumous issues were frequently produced, primarily for the payment of Celtic mercenaries. Imitations of these 'Lysimachi' were also later produced by some of the Celtic tribes. The portrait of Alexander on Lysimachus' coinage, thought to be based on an original work by the famous artist Lysippus, was used as the model for later Hellenistic portraits, too, and the seated Athena design on the reverse was the prototype for many seated goddess figures on Hellenistic, Roman and even later coinages.

## The Hellenistic kingdoms

The archetypal Greek coins of the third century are the regal issues of the major Hellenistic monarchies. There were, however, distinct differences between them. Portraits were used by the Ptolemies and Seleucids, but not by the Antigonids in Macedonia between Demetrius I and Philip V (221–179). Also, while the Seleucid silver coinage usually portrayed the ruling monarch, the Ptolemaic silver usually depicted the dynasty's founder, Ptolemy I.

Portraits of both living and dead kings and queens appeared on issues of Ptolemaic gold coins, further emphasising the dynastic preoccupation of the Macedonian rulers of Egypt. This tradition began under Ptolemy II (285–246) with an issue of gold octadrachms portraying the king and his sister-wife Arsinoe, side by side (jugate) on the obverse, and his parents, Ptolemy I and Berenice I, also jugate and labelled 'gods' (Θεων) on the reverse. Another unusual feature of the Ptolemaic coinage of this period is the production of very large bronze pieces, first introduced under Ptolemy II probably alongside a series of large-denomination gold and silver coins in the name of the deceased and deified Arsinoe. For all the denominations of this bronze coinage the same designs were used:

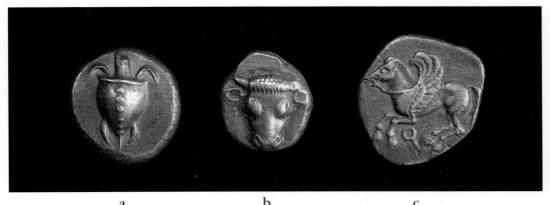

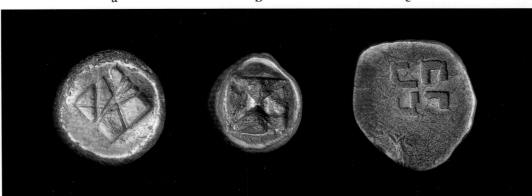

**I–II** Above *Early Greek silver coins, 6th century* BC: (**a**) *'turtle' stater of Aegina;* (**b**) *a bull's head on an Athenian 'wappenmunzen' didrachm;* (**c**) *'Pegasus' on a stater of Corinth. The reverses all have simple punch marks.*

**III** Left *Electrum stater of Cyzicus, 5th century* BC. *On the obverse a kneeling archer tests an arrow for straightness; the reverse has a simple punch mark.*

IV *Detail of 'The Temple of Concord at Agrigentum' (Acragas) by Charles Gore, 1777.*

*V Gold stater of Taras, 4th century* BC, *depicting the boy Taras appealing to his father Poseidon.*

*VI–VII Large bronze coin of Ptolemy* II (285–246 BC), *with a head of Zeus on the obverse and an eagle on a thunderbolt on the reverse.*

**VIII** *African war elephant on a silver coin of the Carthaginians in Spain, late 3rd century* BC.

**IX–X** *Bronze medal by Benedetto Pistrucci, dated 1824, with a trident design copying a bronze coin of Hieron II of Syracuse, Sicily, 3rd century* BC.

a           b           c

41 *Coins of the Ptolemies and the Seleucids:* (a) *gold octadrachm portraying the Ptolemaic dynasty;* (b, c) *silver tetradrachms of Antiochus I, with seated Apollo reverse, and Antiochus III, with elephant reverse.*

VII   head of Zeus on the obverse, eagle(s) on thunderbolt on the reverse. Further issues of huge bronze pieces followed under Ptolemy III (246–222); because Egypt had to import all her silver, there was obvious sense in shifting the currency into metals that were available from lands controlled by the Ptolemies: copper from Cyprus, gold from Nubia. The Ptolemaic coinage was minted in Egypt and in the Ptolemaic possessions of Cyrene, Phoenicia, parts of Asia Minor and Cyprus. Issues were also produced for circulation in Greece during campaigns under Ptolemy I and Ptolemy III.

The Seleucids ruled a vast and unwieldy empire which they endeavoured to control with settlements of Macedonians and Greeks in their many new-founded or refounded cities (often named Antioch or Seleucia), and their coinage was produced from numerous mints from the Aegean coast of Asia Minor in the west to Bactra (Balkh in Afghanistan) in the east. The Seleucids thus pushed the frontiers of Greek coinage further east than ever before. However, theirs was an empire carved out by military conquest; it was incapable of permanent organisation under a Seleucid dynasty that was surrounded by enemies and became racked by internecine struggle. Many of the mints therefore produced Seleucid coinage for only a limited period before the empire gradually disintegrated, though the legacy of Greek-style coinage often survived under the new rulers.

The obverse design on the silver coins of the Seleucids was invariably a portrait of the ruling king; reverse designs were more varied, but a

recurring image used by the dynasty was a figure of Apollo seated on his      41
sacred stone, or omphalos. The portraits are valuable for providing a
gallery of images of Seleucid rulers, including some queens. Some of the
third-century rulers are depicted in a youthful idealised style that would
make them hard to identify without their inscriptions, but there are also
some fine individualised portraits, including those of the most cele-      41
brated member of the dynasty, Antiochus III ('the Great', 223–187),
who attempted to restore Seleucid control over much of the original
empire. It is worth noting that coin portraits have invariably been used
as the basis for identifying ruler portraits in other media; without coins
many ancient sculptures in stone would have remained unidentified.

The third great Hellenistic dynasty, the Antigonids, ruled Macedonia
and dominated much of Greece in the third century. They had to
struggle for their kingdom against intruding rulers – notably King
Pyrrhus of Epirus, most famous for his adventures against Rome, who
had two brief spells in control of Macedon in the 280s and 270s – and
against invading Celtic tribes, but eventually they prevailed. The war
against the Celts is recalled on a coin of Antigonus II Gonatas (276–
239), which has a design of a Macedonian shield on the obverse
containing in its central panel a head of Pan. This is a reference to the      42
Battle of Lysimachia in 277 when the god was believed to have caused
the Gauls to panic. Bronze coins in the name of Antigonus depicting Pan

*42 Silver tetradrachms of the Macedonian kings: (a) Antigonus II Gonatas, with Athena Alkidemos, goddess of Pella, on the reverse; (b) Philip V, club in oak wreath on reverse.*

a                                         b

erecting a trophy provide another reference to this important battle, which secured the kingdom of Macedon for the victor.

Philip v (221–179) reintroduced portraiture to the Macedonian coinage, though only on a brief series of tetradrachms early in his reign. His much more numerous second series depicts Perseus, wearing a Phrygian helmet, in the centre of a Macedonian shield. Philip's devotion to the Argive hero, Perseus, after whom he named his son, born in 217, has been connected to his wife's Argive origins and his own ambitions of conquest. Perseus is also depicted on some of Philip's very abundant bronze coins.

## The Greek cities

Greece was dominated by the Macedonian kingdom for much of the third century, and the Macedonian regal coinage, particularly the lifetime and posthumous issues of Alexander III, provided the main large-denomination currency of the region. However, this was accompanied by a wide range of local or regional coinages with smaller silver denominations struck to various different weight standards and copious amounts of bronze coinage. The most significant local coinages were now produced mainly by leagues of cities. In central and western Greece the Aetolian and Acarnanian Leagues issued coins on both the Attic standard and the local 'Corcyrean' standard. The Attic coins of the Aetolian League bore designs clearly based on the issues of Alexander: the obverse of the tetradrachm has a straight copy of Alexander's Heracles head, while the reverse depicts a seated figure (like Alexander's Zeus), but here it is a (female) personification of Aetolia, seated on a pile of arms including Gallic shields and a Gallic war trumpet. The design celebrates the Aetolians' successful repulsion of the Gallic invasion of 279.

In the Peloponnese the most important power to emerge in the third century was the Achaean League, whose standard coin was the silver hemidrachm (half-drachma), with designs of a head of Zeus on the obverse and the league's monogram on the reverse. The same denomination was also issued by cities in the Peloponnese which were not members of the league; larger coins were rarely minted in this region, but one interesting new producer of Attic-weight tetradrachms was Sparta. The traditions of Greece's most old-fashioned city-state had

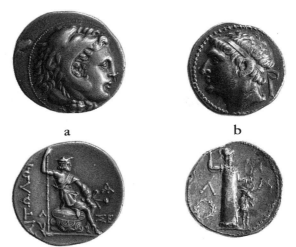

a           b

**43** *Silver coins of Greece:*
**(a)** *Attic-weight
tetradrachm of the Aetolian
League;* **(b)** *tetradrachm of
Sparta with portrait of
king.*

always forbidden precious metal coinage, but in the mid-third century
Sparta at last began to issue small silver obols and, later, tetradrachms.   43
These have been attributed to King Cleomones III in the 220s; a king's
diademed head appears on the obverse, while on the reverse is an archaic
image of Apollo.

On the Asiatic side of the Aegean Sea Alexander tetradrachms, and to
a lesser extent drachms and gold staters, were widely produced, with as
many as twenty-nine cities in Asia Minor striking tetradrachms in the
peak period between 225 and 200. Many of these cities also issued
smaller-denomination local coins in silver and bronze. The island of
Rhodes became a major commercial and political power, retaining its
independence until the first century. Rhodes produced Alexander
tetradrachms and gold Lysimachus staters, but its main production was
in coinage with its own designs in silver didrachms and drachms and   44
bronzes. The head of Helios on Rhodian issues produced after the early
third century is often believed to be based on the head of the famous
colossal statue of Helios – one of the Seven Wonders of the ancient world
– erected at the harbour of Rhodes between 294 and 282 BC to
commemorate the city's successful defence against a siege by Demetrius
Poliorcetes in 305–304. A more bizarre identification given these coins
in the Middle Ages was that the obverse showed Christ with a crown of
thorns (in mistake for the sun's rays of Helios) and the rose was the rose of
Sharon, and these coins then somehow became associated with Judas
Iscariot's thirty pieces of silver! The Rhodian coinage circulated widely

44 *Silver didrachm of Rhodes, 3rd century BC. (2 × actual size)*

and in the late third and early second centuries imitation Rhodian drachms were produced locally in parts of Asia Minor, Crete and Greece, probably in connection with the payment of Rhodian mercenaries.

## The lesser and eastern kingdoms

In Asia Minor there were also several smaller kingdoms issuing their own coinages in the third century. The kingdom of Pergamum was established by the eunuch Philetaerus during the wars of the diadochi. His successors of the Attalid dynasty (named after Attalus, father of Philetaerus) issued coins with a portrait of Philetaerus on the obverse and with a seated Athena, copying the Athena of Lysimachus' coinage, on the reverse. The kingdoms of Bithynia and Pontus in northern Asia Minor, and Cappadocia in the east, all issued their first coins in the mid-third century. Portraits of living rulers in the Seleucid tradition were soon introduced, so their coins provide us with images of their kings.

Further east, new kingdoms were formed from the eastern satrapies of the Seleucid empire which seceded in the course of the third century. For much of the third century the priest-kings of Persis, homeland of the earlier Achaemenid rulers of Persia, issued coins with the usual Hellenistic combination of portrait/seated figure. The silver tetradrachms of Bagadates have a fine Greek-style portrait, but the subject is clearly a non-Greek king, with large moustache and earring, and the seated figure of the king is similarly orientalised. Later issues of Bagadates and the other priest-kings of Persis have a reverse depicting the king standing before the sacred fire of Ahuramazda, a design which later reappeared as standard on the coinage of the Sasanian kings of Persia.

Two much larger kingdoms which emerged in the mid-third century were Parthia and Bactria. The earliest coins of the Parthians may not

a     b     c

45  *Coins of Pergamum,
Persis and Bactria:*
(a) *silver tetradrachm
portraying Philetaerus of
Pergamum, Athena on
reverse;* (b) *silver
tetradrachm of Bagadates,
priest-king of Persis;*
(c) *gold stater of Diodotus
of Bactria, Zeus on reverse.*

have been issued until the early second century, but the rulers of Bactria proclaimed their independence on coins immediately. The first king was Diodotus, previously the Seleucid governor of the Bactrian satrapy. Another Diodotus, presumed to be his son, succeeded him, until he was deposed *c.* 230 by Euthydemus I, who ruled the kingdom until *c.* 200, successfully defending it against the Seleucid king Antiochus III's attempt at reconquest. The names suggest that these rulers were Greeks, and their coins, in gold, silver and bronze, are typically Hellenistic in both content and style. Very little is known of the history of Bactria, so these coins provide precious evidence for this distant outpost of Greek/ Macedonian rule.

45

## The west

The western Greeks were remote from the great events which transformed the eastern Mediterranean in the late fourth and early third centuries, but we have seen already the influence of Alexander and the diadochi on the coins of Agathocles, tyrant of Syracuse 317–289, who used the title 'king' and copied designs from the coins of Alexander for his coinage in the early third century. Around this time the Carthaginians also borrowed from the coinage of Alexander, using his Heracles-head design for their own silver tetradrachms.

46

a          b          c

46 *Silver coins of Sicily and South Italy:* (a) *tetradrachm of the Carthaginians in Sicily;* (b) *didrachm of Pyrrhus, obverse Achilles, reverse Thetis;* (c) *stater of Locri with obverse head of Zeus and reverse depicting Roma and Pistis.*

Another famous historical figure of this period is King Pyrrhus of Epirus, who struck coins in both Italy and Sicily between 280 and 276. Pyrrhus is immortalised in the phrase 'Pyrrhic victory', meaning a victory gained at too great a cost, with reference to the huge losses suffered by his army in defeating the Romans at the Battle of Asculum in 279. Pyrrhus issued coins depicting his legendary ancestors, Achilles and Thetis, perhaps inviting comparisons between his war and the Trojan War, in which Achilles fought against the Trojans, who included Aeneas, legendary ancestor of the Romans. These coins were probably minted for Pyrrhus at Locri in southern Italy; another coin from Locri minted around this time has a more significant design, depicting the personification Pistis ('good faith') crowning a seated Roma and thus declaring the city's loyalty to the emerging 'superpower'.

The Romans themselves began to produce Greek-style coinage around 300 BC, and as their dominance over southern Italy increased the coinages of the Greek cities largely died out, leaving Syracuse in Sicily as the only Greek city in the region with a major coinage in the third century. The other great enemy of the Greeks in the west was Carthage, and it was inevitable that the Carthaginians, with their power bases in western Sicily, Sardinia and Spain, would eventually come into conflict with the Romans. The two major wars between Carthage and Rome in the third century produced some fascinating coinages. In the First Punic War (264–241) the Carthaginians in Sicily issued a series of spectacular large-denomination coins in silver and electrum with the usual Carthaginian design elements of Tanit, horses and palm trees. After the

47 *Coins of Sicily, Spain and Italy:* (a) *silver decadrachm (5 shekels) of the Carthaginians, minted in Sicily;* (b) *silver one-and-a-half shekel piece of the Carthaginians in Spain, with African elephant on the reverse;* (c) *bronze coin of the Brettian League, South Italy.*

defeat of Carthage her mercenary army rebelled, and during this Libyan revolt of 241–238 another numismatic innovation occurred with production of coinage by the rebels in a new alloy, arsenical copper, which was no doubt originally intended to pass as silver. The Second Punic War (218–202) was waged by Hannibal against Rome. Coins issued by the Carthaginians in Spain around this time which have a war elephant on the reverse have been attributed to Hannibal, and the male head on the obverse has been interpreted as a portrait of the great general himself, but it is more likely just a beardless version of the Punic Heracles, Melqart.

During Hannibal's campaign in Italy there was a brief revival of Greek coinage; a significant series was issued in the name of the Brettian League, which allied itself to Hannibal, in gold, silver and bronze. The bronze coins, which are particularly common, include issues with a head of Ares on the obverse and a warlike goddess on the reverse. However, there was to be no lasting revival of Greek coinage in the region; by the end of the century Hannibal was defeated, previously independent Syracuse had been absorbed into the Roman province of Sicily, and Rome was undisputed master not just of Italy but the whole of the western Mediterranean.

# CHAPTER 6

# The Second Century

At the beginning of the second century the great successor kingdoms still held sway over the lands of the eastern Mediterranean. Antiochus III ('the Great') had restored Seleucid control over much of Asia Minor, made gains against the Ptolemies in Phoenicia and Palestine and had ambitiously attempted a reconquest of the east; and the equally energetic Philip V of Macedon had been attacking neighbouring states in the Balkans and the Aegean and posing a sufficient threat for the Romans to contemplate intervention in Greece for the first time. However, the successes of these kings turned out to be short-lived and the only lasting gains were those made by the Romans, whose armies defeated both the Macedonians and the Seleucids, and by the end of the century they controlled Macedonia, Greece and parts of Asia Minor and North Africa, as well as all of the western Mediterranean. Since Greek-style coinages were by now produced throughout all these areas, we can survey the Mediterranean world from west to east to see the perspectives provided by the various coinages.

## The west

In the second century coinage was being produced as far west as Portugal. It had been used in the Iberian peninsula since the fifth century BC, when the first local issues were also made, at the Greek colony of Emporium, and later also at Rhode, both in the Catalonian region of north-east Spain. There had been considerable expansion in the late third century, with native Iberian tribes copying these Greek coinages, and production of 'Punic' coinages in the east and south of Spain by communities of Phoenician origin, including the Carthaginians. Expansion continued in the second century, with the start of the Iberian denarius coinage, the 'Celtiberian' coinages in the interior of

*Coins of western Europe
and North Africa, 2nd
century:* **(a)** *silver drachm of
Emporium, Spain, with
head of Persephone/Pegasus;*
**(b)** *silver drachm of
Massalia, Gaul, Artemis/
lion;* **(c)** *Celtic 'Gallo-
Belgic' gold stater attributed
to the Ambiani;* **(d)** *bronze
coin of Numidia, time of
King Massinissa;* **(e)** *silver
coin of King Vermina,
Mauretania.*

northern Spain, and more mints producing local bronze coinages in the
south. This whole region was now under Roman domination and the
coinages, though locally produced, could be regarded more as 'Roman'
(especially the denarius coinage), though the city of Emporium continued to issue its distinctively Greek coinage of silver drachms and
bronzes.

In Gaul the Greek colony of Massalia went on issuing its coinage in 48
silver – drachms and obols – and bronze even after the Roman conquest
of this part of Gaul in the second century. By this time the Celtic tribes
of the interior were also minting their own coinages. The Greek
prototypes which inspired the coin designs adopted by the Celts of Gaul
(and elsewhere) were mostly those of the cities or states which frequently
employed Celtic mercenaries: Syracuse, Tarentum (Taras), Carthage and
the many users of the Macedonian regal coinage. In Gaul by far the most
popular designs were the Apollo head and chariot of the gold coins of
Philip II of Macedon, which were imitated with varying degrees of
accuracy or imagination. Some of the most wildly barbarous versions
were produced in the second century BC by the 'Gallo–Belgic' tribes in 48
the north.

In Italy and Sicily Roman coinage was by now dominant and the brilliant Greek coinages formerly produced by the independent city-states of the region were just a distant memory. In the second and first centuries only bronze issues were produced. Many cities in Sicily minted these, continuing their independent civic types and their use of Greek inscriptions, but in Italy the only remaining civic mint was Paestum, the former Greek colony of Poseidonia, which now issued small bronze coins with Latin inscriptions. These coins, and the Sicilian civic bronzes, tend to be classified not as 'Greek' but as 'Greek imperial' or 'Roman provincial', since they were produced in a region under direct Roman authority.

Carthage, the long-standing enemy of both the Greeks and the Romans in the western Mediterranean, continued to mint coins after the defeat of Hannibal in 202. No longer produced in Sicily, the coins do not match the fine style of earlier Carthaginian issues, but substantial production was achieved in all metals until it was brought to a sudden end with the Romans' total destruction of the city of Carthage in 146, fulfilling Cato's repeated demand: *'delenda est Carthago'* ('Carthage must be destroyed'). The western neighbours of the Carthaginians were the Numidians, who began striking their first coins in the second century under King Massinissa (202–148). The diademed and bearded head on the obverse of his bronze coins is probably a portrait of Massinissa, while the reverse depicts a galloping horseman. Portrait coins were also minted by the Mauretanian kingdom, to the west of Numidia, where the first issues were produced slightly earlier, under King Syphax (213–202). The coins of his son Vermina, *c.* 200 BC, have a diademed portrait of the king which is very close in style to Ptolemaic coin portraits from Egypt.

## Greece and the Aegean

The second century brought dramatic changes to the coinage of Greece, Macedonia and the Aegean. In Greece the main large silver currency of the previous century had been the Alexander tetradrachms, and the huge output under Alexander and his successors had been supplemented by issues produced by up to eleven Greek cities between 300 and 200 BC. But after 200 BC only one mint, Messene in the Peloponnese, issued

Alexander coins. In Macedonia the dominant silver coinages in the third century had also been the 'Alexanders' and the current issues of the Antigonid kings of Macedonia. The regal Macedonian coinage continued under Philip V after his crushing defeat by the Romans under T. Quinctius Flamininus at the Battle of Cynoscephalae in 197, and under Philip's son Perseus (179–168). However, the Battle of Pydna in 168 brought the Antigonid kingdom to an end and with it the production of independent Macedonian regal coinage.                                     49

Yet Roman domination did not bring Roman coinage to the region. After Flamininus had defeated Philip V and proclaimed the 'freedom' of the Greeks (from the threat of Macedonia) at Corinth in 196, an issue of gold coins was minted bearing his own portrait and a Victory design accompanied by his name in Latin, but this was only an isolated issue and in character it is more 'Greek' than 'Roman'. The coins which emerged as the main new currency of the region were the rejuvenated silver tetradrachms of Athens. These are now referred to as 'New Style' Athenian tetradrachms, but in ancient times they were known as       49 'stephanephori', meaning 'wreath bearers' – a reference to the laurel wreath which surrounds the owl design on the reverse. The wreath is thus the principal difference between these and earlier Athenian tetradrachms, though there were also other changes: Athena's helmet has a triple crest and the owl stands on an overturned amphora. Typical of the coinage of this period, the reverse is also cluttered with inscriptions naming two or three magistrates (at first abbreviated, but later in full), and symbols and numeral letters as additional control marks. These New Style tetradrachms were issued in much larger quantities than any Athenian coins since the fourth century. Numerous inscriptions record quantities of such 'stephanephori', and they appear in hoards throughout the Aegean region and as far west as Italy and east to Syria. They were thus a major regional currency used by many people, including, no doubt, the Romans in Greece and Macedonia. Since the advent of the New Style coinage coincides with the cessation of Macedonian regal coinage, it is possible that much of the silver for this new currency was provided by the recoining of regal issues and 'Alexanders', much of which would have come into Athenian hands through its control of Delos, re-established as a free port in 166.

The wreath border, as used on the New Style tetradrachms, became a

a          b          c

49 *Silver tetradrachms of Greece:* (a) *Perseus, king of Macedon, eagle in oak wreath on reverse;* (b) *Athenian 'New Style' tetradrachm;* (c) *Eretria, Artemis/bull.*

popular accessory to the designs of many Greek coins in the early second century. An oak wreath was used by Philip v and Perseus on their Macedonian coinages, and again when coinage resumed in Macedonia in the name of the four new republics which the Romans established following their overthrow of the kingdom. Wreaths also framed the reverse designs of silver tetradrachms issued in the second century by the Euboean cities of Chalcis and Eretria. The latter coins, which have on the reverse a bull standing within an olive wreath, may be the 'taurophori' (literally 'bull-bearers'; another possibility for these is the coins of an issue of the First Macedonian Republic with Artemis on a bull) recorded in second-century inscriptions from Delos: ' . . . Another [jar] . . . holding 2625 new taurophorus tetradrachms. Another [jar] . . . holding Rhodian [coinage], Attic equivalent 954 drachmas 1 obol. Another [jar] . . . holding Histiaiikon, Attic equivalent 4309 drachmas 3 obols . . .' (*TN* no. 267, from *Inscriptions de Délos*). In this extract the 'Histiaiikon' would be the small, silver, four-obol coins of Histiaea, also in Euboea, which are among the commonest of all late Hellenistic silver coins from Greece. The Rhodian coinage, which continued to be a major currency in the Aegean, would now have mainly been the new 'plinthophori' in drachms and half-drachms. In these Rhodian coins the usual designs of Helios head and rose were framed within a shallow square, giving the appearance of a brick (*plinthos*).

50 *Smaller-denomination coins of Greece, 2nd century:* (a) *silver tetrobol (4 obols) of Histiaea;* (b) *silver hemidrachm (half-drachm) of the Achaean League – the serpent above the monogram on the reverse (attribute of Asklepios, god of healing) identifies the minting city as Epidaurus, of which he was the patron deity;* (c) *silver drachm of the Thessalian League;* (d) *bronze coin of Thespiae in Boeotia.*

In 146 the Romans defeated the Achaean League and destroyed the city of Corinth. This date is usually assumed to mark the end of the important silver coinage (principally in half-drachms) of the Achaean League, though the chronology of this coinage has been disputed on the basis of hoard evidence. The Aetolian League, which had also been a prolific coin producer, was dissolved in 168, but the Thessalian League maintained its output of silver drachms and accompanying bronze issues throughout the second century and indeed for much of the first century. The Thessalian League drachms, which were probably minted at Larissa, have designs of a head of Zeus on the obverse, and on the reverse a standing figure of the Thessalian version of Athena, Athena Itonia, which may copy the statue recorded by the Greek travel writer Pausanias in the second century AD (*Description of Greece* 10.1.10). Otherwise, in the later second century, coinage production in most of the Greek cities was concentrated in bronze issues for purely local circulation.

## Asia Minor

In the early second century the cities of western Asia Minor continued to issue 'Alexander' Attic-weight tetradrachms, and the number of Alexander mints increased after the Romans defeated Antiochus III at the Battle of Magnesia (190) and declared the freedom of the Greek cities of Asia Minor in the Treaty of Apamea in 188. These Alexander coins now have clearly identifiable symbols declaring them to be civic issues, though obviously still using the widely accepted designs of Alexander. However, in the 170s we suddenly see the widespread introduction of Attic tetradrachms by the cities, with new designs apparently emphasis-

51 *Silver coins of Asia Minor:* **(a)** *Alexander tetradrachm minted at Chios (note the sphinx and amphora to the left of the main reverse type);* **(b)** *drachm of Chios, sphinx/amphora;* **(c)** *tetradrachm of Samos, Zeus/cult statue of Hera;* **(d)** *tetradrachm of Myrina with Apollo head and statue;* **(e)** *'cistophoric' tetradrachm of the kingdom of Pergamum.*

ing their independence. These coins usually include the wreath, presumably in imitation of the Athenian 'stephanephori'; on their obverses there is often the city's patron deity and on the reverses a local cult image. Examples of the latter include the statue of Hera at Samos, Artemis Leukophryene at Magnesia and Apollo of Grynium at Myrina.

The island of Tenedos produced an attractive 'wreathed' coinage with particularly intriguing designs which had been used there since the island began coining in the sixth century BC. The obverse has a 'Janiform' head facing both left and right that is, unusually, half-male and half-female. The reverse depicts the *bipennis* ('double axe'), which appears to be the island's badge, plus a series of subsidiary symbols and an inscription naming the island. Various interpretations have been advanced for these designs in both modern and ancient times: '. . . Or rather, as Aristotle says in his Constitution of the Tenedians, because

**52** *Silver tetradrachm of Tenedos. (2 × actual size)*

once a king of Tenedos made a law that anyone who caught adulterers should put them both to death with a double axe. And when his son happened to be caught in the act of adultery, he decreed that the law should be put into effect in the case of his own son. . . . It is for this reason, he says, that on the coinage of the Tenedians a double axe is struck on one side, and on the other two heads, in memory of the fate of the son . . .' Thus Stephanus of Byzantium, writing probably in the early sixth century AD but quoting earlier sources, provides an attractively gruesome, if unlikely, explanation. Modern scholars prefer to believe that the double axe appears in its usual guise as an attribute of Dionysus; it has also been proposed that it recalls the use of axes as a pre-coinage form of money.

Many of the civic coins of western Asia Minor were issued by cities which owed allegiance to the kingdom of Pergamum, which had grown in strength and benefited from siding with Rome against the Macedonian kings and against Antiochus III. In the early second century the regal coinage of the Pergamene kingdom continued, still with a portrait of Philetaerus except for rare examples with the head of Eumenes II (197–158), but in the 170s this was suddenly replaced by a new series, struck to a weight standard that was significantly lower than the previous Attic-weight coinage. The new coins are known as 'cistophori' ('chest-bearers'), so called because of their obverse design of a wicker basket containing snakes used in Dionysiac rituals (the *cista mystica*). Because of their light weight these silver coins could not circulate outside the Pergamene kingdom; the Attalids thus formed a closed

51

currency system like that of Ptolemaic Egypt. It has been proposed that the contemporary civic coins of Attic weight must have been used as international currency by the Pergamene kingdom. In 133 Attalus III bequeathed the Pergamene kingdom to Rome, but the change to Roman administration had little effect on the coinage, as production of 'cistophori' continued under the new rulers without any significant alteration.

The other, lesser kingdoms of Asia Minor retained their independence through the second century. The coinages of the Bithynian and Pontic kingdoms continued much as before, with a regal portrait on the obverse of their tetradrachms and a figure of a deity on the reverse, though one significant new development of importance for their study is the inclusion of dates, which were usually calculated from the foundation of the kingdom. The Cappadocian kingdom, whose third-century coinage had been confined to issues of bronze, began issuing silver tetradrachms under Ariarathes IV (*c.* 220–163). Some of his successors also occasionally issued tetradrachms, but by far the most important denomination in Cappadocia was the drachm. The silver drachms of the Cappadocian kingdom almost invariably have the king's portrait on the obverse and a standing Athena on the reverse, surrounded by inscriptions recording the king's titles and the year of his reign. Because the dates are regnal and not calculated from the foundation of the kingdom, there have been disagreements over the attribution of coins between different kings bearing the same name: ten were called Ariarathes and three Ariobarzanes.

58

## Syria, Egypt and the east

Defeat by the Romans at the Battle of Magnesia in 190 ended Antiochus III's ambitions to restore the Seleucid domain to its original dimensions. Henceforth, Seleucid influence in Asia Minor was much reduced, but the dynasty continued to rule Syria, Palestine and, until mid-century, many lands further east. With the gradual diminution of the Seleucid kingdom and its collapse into near-anarchy through internecine warfare, a strong and stable coinage would not be expected. However, the proliferation of rival claimants to the throne does give the Seleucid coinage of the second century diversity and considerable historical interest.

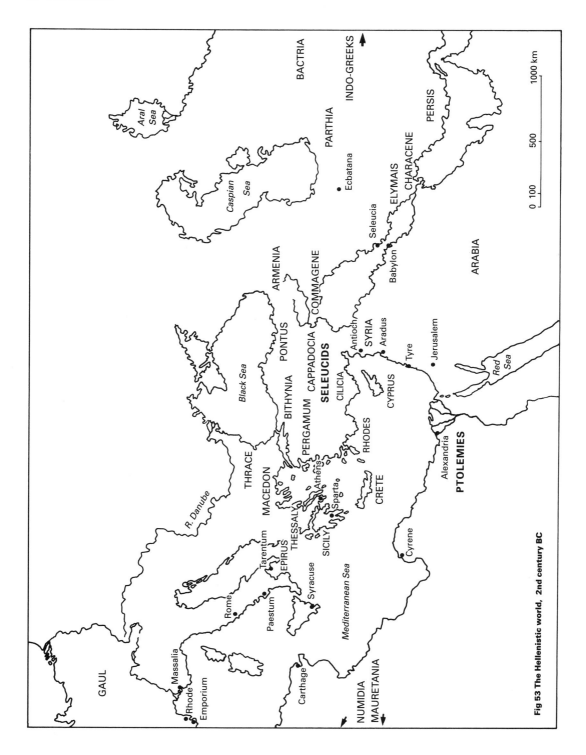

**Fig 53 The Hellenistic world, 2nd century BC**

53 Opposite *The Hellenistic kingdoms, 2nd century BC.*

54 *Silver tetradrachms of the Seleucid kings of Syria:* (a) *Antiochus IV;* (b) *Antiochus VI;* (c) *Demetrius II, mint of Tarsus;* (d) *Antiochus VIII.*

The tradition of ruler portraits was well embedded in the coinage of the Seleucids, so we are provided with portraits of all the successors of Antiochus III. They are usually adorned with just a diadem, as can be seen from the example of Antiochus IV (175–164) illustrated. Competent but cruel, this Antiochus gained particular infamy for his brutal suppression of a Jewish revolt, which included sacking the Temple of Jerusalem. The Jews had rebelled because of Antiochus' attempt to introduce the worship of Zeus in Jerusalem, and he himself assumed the title 'Theos Epiphanes' ('God Manifest'), though this was jokingly changed to 'Epimanes' ('Crazy') by some of his subjects. Antiochus was also portrayed on some of his coins as the sun-god Helios, but the most striking example of such a manifestation is the portrait on silver tetradrachms of the boy-king Antiochus VI, called 'Epiphanes Dionysus' (145–142). There is still a marked individuality in these Seleucid portraits. Further examples include Demetrius II, whose portrait in his second reign (129–125), following a lengthy period of captivity in

Parthia, seems to show an adoption of oriental fashion, and Antiochus VIII (126–96, another 'Epiphanes'), who was nicknamed Grypus ('Hook-nosed') for obvious reasons.  54

The principal change to the design of Seleucid coins in the second century was the introduction of longer inscriptions, to incorporate the extended titles of the kings – for example, 'Epiphanes', or the equally self-deluding 'Nicator' ('Victor') or 'Soter' ('Saviour'). From the middle of the century dates were also included, calculated from the beginning of the Seleucid era, 312 BC, as well as mint marks, and the whole reverse design, and the obverse portrait, were enclosed within a border delineated by pellets, more elaborate beading or a wreath (following contemporary fashion). The principal reverse design on the silver tetradrachms was normally a seated or standing god, usually Apollo or Zeus, though Phoenician mints also used an eagle design borrowed from the Ptolemies; designs on the bronze coins were much more varied and often of significance to the mint city. An interesting development on certain Seleucid bronze issues was the use of coin flans with serrated edges. This was popular for a time in mid-century and the fashion even spread to Rome, where it appeared on some silver denarii.

In the early second century there were still numerous mints producing Seleucid coinage, from Asia Minor in the west to Ecbatana (in Iran) in the east, but most of the eastern mints were lost with the Parthian conquest of all the Seleucid lands east of Mesopotamia under Mithradates I (c. 171–138). Seleucid coinage continued in Syria and neighbouring areas: Cilicia to the north-west, Phoenicia to the south; but before the end of the century the more powerful cities, such as Aradus, Sidon and  55 Tyre, were also striking autonomous silver coinages. It was also in this period that production of a Judaean coinage resumed, apparently following authorisation granted by Antiochus VII (138–129) according to the Bible: '. . . and I permitted you your own striking, coinage for your country' (I Maccabees 15, 6).

The Ptolemaic coinage shows a marked decline in the second century. The evidence of papyri indicates that between 183 and 173 the price of silver in Egypt escalated to the extent that its value against bronze increased from 1:60 to 1:480. It is surely not a coincidence that this was also the period when silver coinages elsewhere, notably in Macedonia and Pergamum, were reduced in weight. There was obviously a general

shortage of silver that was particularly acute in Egypt; most of the silver Ptolemaic tetradachms were now struck in Cyprus or Phoenicia, while coinage production at Alexandria concentrated mainly on bronze issues. The previously plentiful Ptolemaic gold coinage also becomes exceedingly scarce after Ptolemy V (205–180), and so only rarely are we provided with portraits of living rulers, since the silver coinage usually continued to portray Ptolemy I (except for some Phoenician issues), and the bronze coins still avoided portraits. One exceptional gold octadrachm portrays the young Ptolemy VI soon after his accession in 180 with his mother Cleopatra I (daughter of Antiochus the Great), who ruled as regent until her death in 176.

As the Seleucid empire shrank, new kingdoms emerged in the east ruled by non-Greeks, but these people all inherited coinage from the Seleucids and their early issues, at least, belong in the Greek coinage tradition. Parthian coinage began around 200 BC or perhaps earlier; since the ruling king was not named on the coins, many of the issues are notoriously difficult to date, though the silver Parthian tetradrachms and many bronze coins were dated according to the Seleucid era. The tetradrachms were mostly struck at the mint of Seleucia on the River Tigris, which was incorporated into the Parthian kingdom following the conquest of Mesopotamia *c.* 138 by Mithradates I. The inscriptions in Greek and the reverse design of a seated deity based on the Seleucid Apollo figure emphasise the Greek ancestry of these coins. Some of the

55 *Coins of* (a) *Phoenicia,* (b) *Egypt and* (c, d) *Parthia:* (a) *silver tetradrachm of Aradus, 133/2 BC, city goddess/ Nike;* (b) *Egyptian gold octadrachm of Cleopatra I and Ptolemy VI;* (c) *silver tetradrachm of Mithradates I;* (d) *silver drachm of Mithradates II.*

56 *Silver coins of Bactrian and Indo-Greek kings:* **(a)** *Demetrius I, Heracles on reverse;* **(b)** *Antimachus, Poseidon reverse;* **(c)** *Eucratides I, dioscuri (Castor and Pollux) reverse;* **(d)** *Agathocles, imitating the coinage of Alexander the Great;* **(e)** *Menander.*

early portraits on Parthian coins also have a quite 'Greek' style, but during the reign of Mithradates II (123–91) the character of the portrait assumes a much more elaborate oriental appearance including a decorated domed headdress. On the silver drachms, which were the main coins of the Parthians, there are also Greek inscriptions, but the seated archer reverse type on these coins is purely Parthian.

Further east the kingdom of Bactria prospered for a while as an outpost of Greek civilisation. King Demetrius (*c.* 200–190) extended the kingdom eastwards into the Punjab; hence he is portrayed on coins as a conqueror of India, with elephant-scalp headdress similar to that used for the portraits of Alexander the Great under Ptolemy I. Demetrius'

eastern conquests later formed a separate Indo-Greek kingdom, which
outlasted the original Bactrian kingdom following the latter's overthrow
by a nomad invasion *c*. 140 BC. The Bactrian and Indo-Greek kings were
obviously aware of their isolation from the rest of the Greek world, and
they reacted by emphasising their western origins on their coins. Thus
Antimachus (*c*. 185–170) wears the Macedonian flat cap, or kausia, and
Eucratides I (*c*. 170–145) wears a helmet adorned with the bull's horn of
Poseidon, and reverse designs depict Greek gods and heroes: Athena,
Zeus, Apollo, Artemis, Poseidon, Heracles and the dioscuri. The Indo-
Greek king Agathocles (*c*. 190–180) even issued a series of coins
portraying famous Greeks, including Antiochus III and Alexander the
Great; but at the same time bronze coins were also produced which
clearly incorporate native Indian influences – square in shape, with
Indian deities and Brahmi or Kharosthi inscriptions (as well as Greek).
Most of the Bactrian and Indo-Greek kings are obscure figures, and some
are known only from their coins, but one king who penetrated both
western and Indian literature was King Menander (*c*. 165–130). On the
tetradrachm of Menander illustrated, the king's portrait and titles in
Greek appear on the obverse, while the reverse depicts a Greek goddess,
Athena Alkidemos of Pella, but has an inscription in Kharosthi.

# CHAPTER 7

# The First Century

The history of the first century BC is dominated by Rome, which produced a succession of warlords: Sulla, Pompey, Crassus, Julius Caesar, Mark Antony and Octavian, who all fought in the eastern Mediterranean against foreign kings, or against each other. The Greeks could provide no heroes to match these, though two eastern kings, Mithradates VI of Pontus and Tigranes II of Armenia, earned the title 'the Great' through their military successes against Rome or her allies. Eventually, however, all of the eastern Mediterranean lands, including the remaining successor kingdoms of Seleucid Syria and Ptolemaic Egypt, were absorbed into the Roman Empire, which by the end of the century had been extended almost to its furthest limits. This is therefore the final chapter in the story of independent Greek coinage.

## The west

In the western Mediterranean Greek coinage had virtually disappeared by the first century. The only remaining 'Greek' mint was probably Massalia in southern Gaul, which continued to issue its famous silver drachms and fractions until mid-century. In this period native (usually Celtic) tribes in Gaul also produced numerous coinages which were ultimately derived from Greek prototypes, but these too were about to give way to the advance of Rome. In Spain, meanwhile, local bronze coinage continued through the first century, but the gradual adoption of Latin inscriptions confirms the Roman character of these coinages, paving the way for their later replacement by purely Roman coinage. A similar process was also underway in Italy and Sicily, where the areas previously rich in Greek coinages (or their native imitations) were confined to just a few local bronze issues, and these too were completely Romanised by the end of the Republican period.

In North Africa the Roman province formed after the destruction of Carthage in 146 used Roman coinage, and even outside the Roman province Roman coinage had become supreme by the mid-first century. Thus, when Juba I of Numidia (60–46) and Bogud, king of Mauretania (49–38), issued coins, they struck Roman denominations, mostly silver denarii. The denarii of Juba I portray the king like a Hellenistic Greek monarch, but his name is inscribed in Latin, and the acceptability of these coins as denarii is confirmed by their appearance in Roman denarius hoards. The many civic bronze coinages of North Africa in the first century should also be regarded as local coins within the Roman sphere, akin to the later 'Greek imperial' bronzes of the eastern Roman Empire.

## Greece and Asia Minor

East of the Adriatic Sea independent Greek coinages did survive into the first century. The cities of Apollonia and Dyrrhachium in Illyria had been producing a substantial coinage in silver drachms since the third century. This coinage, which circulated widely in western Greece and north into the Danube region, was undoubtedly used by the Roman military in the area and has also been linked with the trade in Celtic slaves. The designs on the drachms of both cities are essentially the same: a cow suckling a calf on the obverse, and a patterned square on the reverse – a combination that had been used on coins from this part of western Greece, including Corcyra (Corfu), for 400 years. Production eventually ceased at both mints mid-century, the final issues probably produced in connection with the Civil War between Pompey and Caesar, 49–48 BC.

The drachms of Apollonia and Dyrrhachium did not circulate in southern Greece. Here, the main silver coinage continued to be the New Style tetradrachms of Athens. This was clearly the official coinage of the Roman province of Achaea (all of Greece south of Thessaly), and output continued until the 40s BC. The most interesting issues of the first century are the silver tetradrachms, and associated gold coins, in the name of 'King Mithradates': these date from 88–86 BC when the supporters of Mithradates VI of Pontus held Athens. At the same time, imitation New Style tetradrachms were produced by Mithradates' opponent, the famous Roman general Lucius Cornelius Sulla, who

**57** *Silver coins:*
**(a)** *denarius of King Juba I of Numidia, temple on reverse;* **(b)** *drachm of Dyrrhachium;* **(c)** *tetradrachm of Macedonia in the name of Aesillas, Roman governor;* **(d)** *tetradrachm of Thasos with a young head of Dionysus and a standing Heracles;* **(e)** *late 'posthumous' Alexander tetradrachm minted at Odessus.*

retook Athens in 86 (and sacked the city). There does not appear to have been any production of small-denomination silver coinage in southern Greece at this time, but bronze issues are plentiful; they presumably provided the local currency for each city.

To the north of Achaea, Thessaly's league coinage continued well into the first century. The final issues again probably belong to the Civil War, which culminated in the defeat of Pompey at Pharsalus in Thessaly in 48 BC. Further north, the Roman province of Macedonia had its own issues of silver tetradrachms; by far the largest was the last series struck in the name of the Roman quaestor Aesillas, probably to pay the costs of an earlier war, against Mithradates, in 87–86 BC. For these coins the designs are: obverse, head of Alexander the Great; reverse, club, money chest and quaestor's chair of office. The appearance of Alexander's portrait is interesting – the Roman authorities adopting a past Macedonian hero for their provincial coinage. In Macedonia, as in Greece, the Roman denarius gradually became more common, and replaced the local silver coinages from mid-century. Local Greek bronze issues continued, but these should now be regarded as Roman provincial coins.

57

Two other Greek silver coinages which survived into the first century were struck in Thrace. These were the tetradrachms of Maroneia and Thasos, produced in large quantities since the mid-second century. The last posthumous Alexander and Lysimachus tetradrachms (and Lysimachus gold staters), produced in mints in the Black Sea region, also spluttered into the early first century, but then ceased forever. One of the last 'Alexanders', from the mint of Odessus, *c.* 75 BC, has a Heracles head which is given the unmistakable features of Mithradates VI.

Mithradates was one of the most extraordinary characters of the Hellenistic age. During his reign of nearly sixty years he led Greek resistance against Roman oppression, even though, as his name suggests, he belonged to a non-Greek dynasty. The appearance of his portrait on an Alexander tetradrachm is particularly apt, since a change of portrait style on his own coins (from realistic to more youthful and idealised) suggests that Mithradates wished to promote himself as a sort of latter-day Alexander. This change of portraiture took place around the time that Mithradates began his war against the Romans, in 89 BC, and the new youthful portrait remained on his coins for the rest of his reign. In addition to silver tetradrachms Mithradates also issued gold staters, and many city coinages from Pontus with shared designs clearly belong to his reign, with some of the designs quite pointedly referring to Mithradates. An important innovation to base-metal coinage can also be dated to the reign of Mithradates. This was the introduction of a new alloy, brass, known to the ancients as orichalcum, which was first used for coinage in Pontus at this time.

Mithradates was in the end unsuccessssful and the legacy of his uprising in Asia Minor was the imposition by Sulla of a crippling indemnity which must have impoverished the cities. At the same time Roman influence over what remained of the local coinages seems to have increased. Various cities in Asia Minor had continued to produce cistophoric tetradrachms under Roman rule. Production ceased in 67 BC, but then resumed again in 58 BC with issues that now carried the names of the local Roman governor and of the city magistrates responsible for their production. Roman governors' names also appeared on bronze coins issued by cities in the new Roman province of Bithynia and Pontus, which was formed in 63 BC after the former independent kingdom of Bithynia had been bequeathed to the Romans.

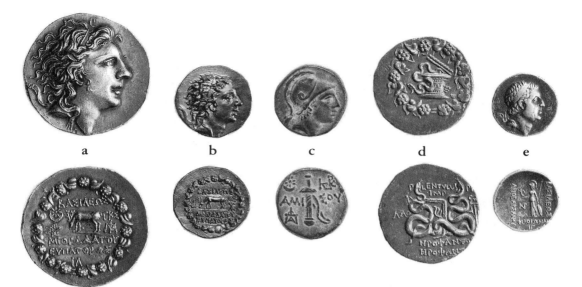

58 *Coins of Asia Minor:*
**(a, b)** *silver tetradrachm and gold stater of Mithradates VI of Pontus, grazing stag in ivy wreath on reverse;* **(c)** *bronze coin of Amisus in Pontus, time of Mithradates VI;* **(d)** *'cistophoric' tetradrachm with the name of the Roman governor Lentulus, minted at Laodicea in Phrygia, 56–53 BC;* **(e)** *silver drachm of Ariobarzanes I ('Philoromaios') of Cappadocia.*

A few cities in Asia Minor produced their own issues of silver coinage in the first century (some in any case were probably connected with Roman military operations), but these gradually came to an end. Roman denarii began to circulate in Asia Minor in the time of the Civil Wars and the few Greek silver coinages (for example, the cistophori and the drachms of Lycia) and the many city bronze coinages that survived into the Roman Empire should be regarded as local variations of the Roman coinage system, rather than as independent Greek coinages.

The Cappadocian kingdom, like the Bithynian, had become a client of Rome, and the pro-Roman attitude of King Ariobarzanes I (95–62) is reflected in his Roman-style portrait on coins. It has been argued that this type of portrait was deliberately chosen to emphasise characteristics akin to those promoted by contemporary Roman portraits – middle-aged, care-worn and serious – in contrast to the youthfulness, idealism and flamboyance of the Mithradates portrait. Mithradates repeatedly expelled Ariobarzanes from his kingdom, but the Romans always restored their 'friend' (*Philoromaios*).

58

## Syria, the east and Egypt

East of Cappadocia were more kingdoms which had earlier broken away from the Seleucid Empire. Commagene was another client kingdom of

Rome for much of its existence; its coinage, which spans the late second century BC to the mid-first century AD, mostly consisted of issues of bronze. Armenia, on the other hand, provided another of Rome's great opponents in the first century, King Tigranes II (95–56). An ally of Mithradates VI, whose daughter he married, he expanded the Armenian kingdom for a time to include Commagene and Syria. The earliest Armenian coins, which are all of bronze, probably date from his reign, and during his occupation of Syria (83–69) he minted silver tetradrachms. These have a fine portrait on the obverse of Tigranes wearing an Armenian tiara, and on the reverse they depict the statue of Tyche of Antioch, with the river-god Orontes at her feet – a statue recorded by the Greek writer Pausanias as being by the famous sculptor Eutychides of Sicyon.

The coins of the many Seleucid kings of Syria in the early first century have a dull formalised appearance. The portraits differ only in minor details, though the kings' titles and changing reverse designs confirm the identifications which provide us with a sequence for the separate contestants still fighting for control of their shrinking kingdom. Typifying the situation is a tetradrachm of Antiochus XI and his twin brother Philip I, joint rulers in Antioch for just a few weeks in 95 BC before Antiochus drowned in the River Orontes. Three more of their brothers, Seleucus VI, Demetrius III and Antiochus XII, and a cousin, Antiochus X, each ruled parts of the kingdom within the decade 95–85 BC. Philip I

a    b    c

59 *Silver tetradrachms of Syria:* (a) *Tigranes the Great of Armenia, minted at Antioch;* (b) *Seleucid kings Antiochus XI and Philip I;* (c) *pseudo-Philip coin issued under the Romans, 46/5 BC.*

**60** *Silver shekel of Tyre, dated 61 BC.*
*(2 × actual size)*

'Philadelphus' ('Brother-lover', an ironic title for any Seleucid king) ruled long enough altogether to produce a coinage which was later copied by the Roman rulers of Syria, following the final overthrow of the Seleucid kingdom by Pompey in 64 BC. This 'pseudo-Philip' coinage was introduced by the Roman governor Gabinius in 57 BC; in appearance the coins are late Seleucid, but they were the local silver coins for the     59 Roman province of Syria.

In the meantime the free cities of Syria and Phoenicia produced substantial coinages in silver and bronze, or just in bronze. Particularly important were the silver shekels of Tyre, which circulated throughout     60 Phoenicia and also in Palestine where they were used for paying the Jewish temple tax. The Jews were by now striking their own coins in Jerusalem under their Hasmonaean rulers, beginning with Alexander     61 Jannaeus (103–76 BC). Only bronze coins were issued and the designs (lacking portraits because Jewish law forbade human representation) borrow some of their imagery, notably the anchor, from Seleucid bronze coins. The neighbouring Arab kingdom of Nabataea, based in Jordan, also began minting coins in the first century. Hellenistic-style portraits and Greek inscriptions (later Aramaic) were used for the issues in silver and bronze.

61 *Eastern coins:* (a) *bronze coin of Alexander Jannaeus, Hasmonaean ruler of Judaea;* (b) *silver tetradrachm of King Kamnaskires II and Queen Anzaze of Elymais;* (c) *tetradrachm of King Attambelos of Characene, dated year 272 (41/40 BC);* (d) *silver drachm of Orodes II of Parthia.*

Further east, other native kingdoms also inherited the Hellenistic coinage tradition. Elymais and Characene, two kingdoms at the head of the Persian Gulf, both at first produced silver tetradrachms strongly influenced (like the Parthian coinage) by the Seleucids: King Kamnaskires II and Queen Anzaze of Elymais are portrayed together, diademed, on the obverse of a tetradrachm of 82/81 BC, with a seated Zeus on the reverse; while King Attambelos of Characene, diademed, but with dread-locked long hair and beard, has a seated Heracles on the reverse of his tetradrachm of 41/40 BC, and the coin has Greek inscriptions and is dated by the Seleucid era. The Parthian coinage continued as before, but was growing gradually more formalised and oriental. A typical mid-first-century drachm portrays Orodes II whose armies inflicted one of the greatest-ever defeats on the Romans with their massacre of the legions of Crassus at Carrhae in 53 BC.

Meanwhile in the distant east the Indo-Greek kings continued to issue their coins. In the first century these were bilingual, and native Indian influences are also evident in some designs and in the fabric and weights of bronze issues. However, portraits and Greek designs continued to the end of the series, around the middle of the century, and were then also taken over by the Scythian and Parthian rulers of the region.

Returning to the eastern Mediterranean, it is appropriate to conclude this historical survey of Greek coinage with the coins of the Ptolemies, whose last ruler was also their most famous – Queen Cleopatra VII (51–

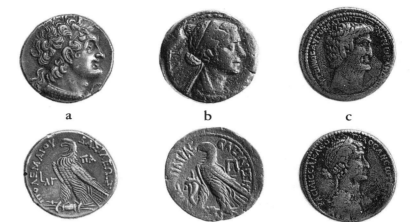

a                    b                    c

**62** *Late Ptolemaic coins:*
**(a)** *Ptolemy* VIII, *year 33;*
**(b)** *bronze coin of Cleopatra*
VII; **(c)** *silver shekel of*
*Antony and Cleopatra*
*minted in Phoenicia.*

30 BC). In the early first century the Ptolemaic silver and bronze coinage was as characterless as that of the late Seleucids, but without the interest provided by portraits of the living ruler, since the silver tetradrachms continued to depict an idealised head of Ptolemy I. However, Cleopatra's 62 portrait appears on several issues of coinage, including bronzes from the mint of Alexandria and silver tetradrachms from Ascalon. An issue of 62 bronze from Cyprus uniquely portrays her with the baby Caesarion, son of Julius Caesar, and we are reminded of another of her liaisons when she is portrayed on Phoenician shekels which have Mark Antony's head on 62 the other side.

CHAPTER 8

# The Legacy of Greek Coins

T he Hellenistic age formally came to a close with the death of
Queen Cleopatra in 30 BC, but this was not the end of the story
of Greek coinage. Under the Roman Empire the Greek cities
or kingdoms were all either subject or client states, and their coins are
now classified as 'Greek imperial' or 'Roman provincial'; however, in
cultural terms they are often just as 'Greek' as earlier independent issues.
The non-Greek kingdoms beyond the control or influence of Rome also
issued coinages which can no longer be classified as Greek, but often
Greek influences from their origins can still be detected. Finally, and
perhaps most important of all, the Roman conquerors of the Greek world
inevitably absorbed into their own coinage aspects of the Greek coins
they encountered, so that consciously or not they nursed the Greek
tradition and eventually passed it on to others.

## The continuing history of Greek coins

So-called 'Greek imperial' coins were produced by hundreds of city
mints, mainly in the eastern half of the Roman Empire, from the first
century BC to the late third century AD. These coins have traditionally
been classified under the heading 'Greek' since they were issued by
predominantly Greek communities for local or regional circulation and
their inscriptions were usually in Greek, though the epithet 'imperial'
refers, of course, to the Roman (not a Greek) Empire. Because the great
majority of these coins were struck in base metals, and hence are less
valuable to collectors and more likely to be worn or corroded, and
because of their 'late' (in ancient Greek terms) date, they have traditionally been considered the poor relations of earlier Greek coins –
chronologically they appear in *Historia Numorum* after the groups listed
under the dismissive heading 'Period of Continued Decline in Art'!

However, more recently there has been a tendency for these coins to be studied in their historical context, and a growing appreciation of the contribution they can make to an understanding of political, economic and cultural life in the empire is helping their rehabilitation as 'Roman provincial'.

Most 'Greek imperial' coins are the direct descendants of the earlier civic coins, though some derived from the coinages of Hellenistic kingdoms: for example, the silver cistophori of the Roman province of Asia from the Attalid coinage of Pergamum, and the coinages of Roman client kingdoms, such as Pontus and Herodian Judaea, from earlier independent or Seleucid-client dynastic coinages. On 'Greek imperial' coins the head of the ruling Roman emperor was usually given pride of place on the obverse, and there are also sometimes references to the emperor or other members of the imperial family on reverses.

However, the real value of the designs on 'Greek imperial' coins lies in what they can reveal about the cities themselves. Local architecture and topography are depicted, and cultural events or practices, including local religious cults, mythology or civic celebrations (sometimes involving alliances between cities – an ancient form of 'twinning'), are recorded. In this way the coins were used as vehicles for expressing civic pride, and because they tended to use a wider variety of designs than in earlier periods they can be more revealing than Classical or Hellenistic Greek coins. They provide more depictions of Greek art and architecture, including images of famous statues, such as the Aphrodite of Cnidus by Praxiteles or Pheidias' statue of Zeus at Olympia, and a view  63 of the Acropolis of Athens. Altogether, some 800 different buildings are  63 depicted on Greek coins, but the vast majority appear only on 'Greek imperials'. A good example is the famous Temple of Artemis at Ephesus. This was, like Pheidias' Zeus, another of the Seven Wonders of the World, but it was not depicted on coins of Ephesus until the Roman  63 period. The image from these bronze coins has in modern times been used to draw reconstructions of the great temple, which in turn were copied by the surrealist artist Salvador Dali in his painting 'The Temple of Diana at Ephesus'. Graphic illustrations from mythology also appear on 'Greek imperial' coins, including an imaginative yet quaint depiction of Leander swimming across the Hellespont towards his lover Hero on a coin of Abydus in Troas, Asia Minor. Also from Troas are coins of Ilium  63

63 *Greek imperial bronze coins (reverse designs):* **(a)** *Cnidus in Caria, statue of Aphrodite;* **(b)** *Athens, the Acropolis;* **(c)** *Ephesus, the Temple of Artemis;* **(d)** *Abydus, Hero and Leander;* **(e)** *Ilium, Hector in a chariot;* **(f)** *Alexandria in Troas, Alexander taming Bucephalus.*

showing scenes from that most famous of Greek legends, the Trojan War, and coins of Alexandria Troas illustrating events from the life of the king after whom the city was named, Alexander the Great. In this way the Greek cities under the Roman Empire celebrated their mythology and history through coinage, and by thus expressing their own antiquarian interests they have left for us a precious heritage in these bronze coins.

In the eastern kingdoms beyond the reach of Rome, the tendency for the coinages to 'go native', which was already under way in the Hellenistic period, continued apace. On the coins of the Parthians and their Sasanian successors in Iran and of the Kushanas and their successors further east, local scripts replaced the earlier Greek and local artistic styles took over the designs. The coming of Islam furthered this process with the general elimination of depictions of human figures and their replacement with designs restricted to Arabic inscriptions. However, occasional issues with pictorial designs sometimes reappeared under less orthodox Islamic dynasties, and a distant echo of a Classical Greek coin design (the facing head of Arethusa from Syracuse) can be seen in a twelfth-century bronze coin issued by Zengid rulers in Iraq.

Meanwhile the Romans may have conquered the Greeks, but even the

64 *Bronze coin of Sayf al-Din Ghazi* II, *Zengid ruler of Mosul,* AD 1170–80, *with obverse design of facing head ultimately derived from Greek coins.*

Romans were prepared to admit that they were themselves conquered by Greek culture, a fact of which the coinage of the Roman Empire provides clear proof. Some imperial coins have reverse designs clearly copying Greek prototypes from the fifth to fourth centuries BC, but generally the principal influence was the coinage of the Hellenistic kings. Most Roman imperial coins depict a head of the ruling emperor on the obverse and a figure of a god, seated or standing as on Hellenistic coins, or a personification of a virtue representing the values of imperial rule ('Courage', 'Honesty', 'Liberality' and so on) on the reverse. After several centuries this tradition was then passed on to the Byzantine Empire in

65

65 *The Greek tradition in Roman and later coins:* (a, b) *silver denarii of Augustus with designs copying coins of Thurii and Neapolis (compare figs 19b, 31a, c); sestertii of* (c) *Nero and* (d) *Antoninus Pius, with figures of Roma and Britannia based on Greek designs of a seated Athena (compare fig. 39b);* (e) *copper farthing of Charles* II, 1671, *with Britannia design following the same tradition.*

the eastern Mediterranean and to the barbarian kingdoms which replaced Rome in the west, and thence to the states of medieval Europe. Christianity had in the interim imposed its own styles and symbols, and over the centuries the Graeco-Roman original was transformed into a rather different coin, but the revival of naturalistic art in the Renaissance brought a restoration of the earlier tradition on the coinage. Naturalistic portraits reappeared and the increased size of coin flans prompted a revival of more imaginative reverse designs, which sometimes looked back to earlier examples for inspiration. Thus, for example, we can see that in the British farthing of the seventeenth century the Britannia figure is clearly based on a Roman Britannia originating in the second century AD, which itself borrows from similar figures of Roma, that are themselves descended from the Athena on Hellenistic coins of Lysimachus.

The long history of Greek coinage concludes with examples of modern coins imitating ancient Greek originals. Not surprisingly, the modern state of Greece has used ancient Greek coins as the inspiration for some of its coin designs. These have included a head of Demeter copied from fourth-century BC coins of the Amphictionic Council, coupled with the corn-ear from coins of Metapontum, and a design of Thetis on a sea-horse copied from coins of King Pyrrhus of Epirus.

66 *Greek coins of the 20th century:* **(a)** 10 *drachmas, 1930 (compare figs 27b, 8b);* **(b)** *drachma, 1910 (compare fig. 46b).*

## Greek coins and art

The modern copying of images from ancient Greek coin designs has been facilitated by the publication of ancient Greek coins, with photographs, in numerous books and catalogues since the nineteenth century. However, the academic study of ancient coins has been progressing for centuries, and the impact of numismatic study on art in general, as well as on coinage, should be noted.

There was an awareness of ancient Greek and (more especially) Roman coins in the Middle Ages. The Holy Roman Emperor Frederick II (1215–50) issued coins, known as 'Augustales', in South Italy with portraits based on coin portraits of the Roman emperor Augustus. From the same region and the same period comes a cameo with a familiar Classical design of Heracles and the Nemean lion which may ultimately derive from the ancient coins of Heraclea. Collectors of ancient coins in the Middle Ages included Petrarch in Italy and Jean, Duc de Berry, in France, and many more emerged in the Renaissance, when we also see frequent quotations from ancient art, including Greek and Roman coins, being incorporated into the art of the period. The clearest examples of coin-copying appear in the cast bronze medals of Antonio Pisano ('Pisanello', c. 1395–1455), Leone Leoni (1509–90) and others, but images borrowed from coins could also be projected on to larger works in relief sculpture or painting by artists with antiquarian interests like Andrea Mantegna (c. 1431–1506) and Pirro Ligorio (c. 1500–83). The ancient coins providing the inspiration were almost always Roman imperial, rather than Greek, though there were a few exceptions. The Greek coin influences most readily available in Renaissance Italy were the surviving coins of the ancient Greek cities of South Italy and Sicily. Thus Valerio Belli (1468–1546) and Giovanni Cavino (1500–70), who

67

67 *Medals with designs based on ancient Greek coins:* (a) *'after the antique' medal by Valerio Belli (compare fig. 17a);* (b, c) *French medals of the Napoleonic period:* (b) *conquest of Naples, 1806, medal by Nicholas Brenet (compare fig. 31a);* (c) *conquest of Illyria, 1809, medal by Alexis Depaulis (compare fig. 57b).*

specialised in producing medals imitating ancient coins, copied the
Syracusan decadrachm of Euainetos. Cavino also produced an imaginary
draped bust of Queen Artemisia of Caria (wife of Maussolus) which may
have been inspired by a bust of a Ptolemaic queen from a coin, but the
majority of his work, typical of sixteenth-century classicising, copied
Roman imperial originals.

Roman coins continued to be more influential than Greek coins in the
work of later artists; for instance, Rubens' drawings 'after the antique'
include clear copies of Roman imperial coin portraits but no direct copies
of genuine Greek coins. However, in the early nineteenth century we can
find unmistakable copies of Greek coins. French medals celebrating the
conquests of Naples and Illyria by Napoleon's armies copied ancient
Greek coins of the same localities, and in 1825 Eugène Delacroix
published a series of lithographs of ancient Greek coins which are so
detailed that the individual specimens being copied, from the French
national collection or the collection of the Duc de Blacas (later acquired
by the British Museum), can be identified. The philhellenism that
inspired Delacroix was just as evident in Britain in this period. In 1824
Benedetto Pistrucci produced a medal in honour of George IV, portraying the king diademed like a Hellenistic monarch and with inscriptions

**68** *Lithograph by
Delacroix, 'Twelve Antique
Coins', 1825: Greek coin
types copied include those of
Tenedos (compare fig. 52),
Carthage (compare fig. 47a)
and Aenus (compare fig.
20e). Note that images on
the lithograph are reversed.*

in Greek. On the reverse is a trident-and-dolphins design copied from
the bronze coins of Hieron II of Syracuse (275–216 BC). As with the
drawings of Delacroix, the details are so clear and precise that it is
possible to identify the individual coin being copied (one which was
certainly in the British Museum collection in Pistrucci's time); and
thirty-five years later the exact same design reappeared on a pattern
decimal penny produced by the Royal Mint. The influence of Greek
coins on sculpture and painting is more difficult to identify with
certainty. Were, for instance, the 'Grecian maidens' in the paintings of
Albert Moore – or of Lord Leighton, Poynter, or Alma-Tadema –
influenced at all by female heads on Greek coins? We cannot be sure, but
it seems unlikely that these nineteenth-century artists, obviously inter-
ested in Greek and Roman subjects, could have avoided being influenced
by the numerous images of Greek coins available by their time.

## Greek numismatics

Since the Renaissance ancient coins have also been of particular interest
to historians. At first their usual purpose was to provide images to add
visual impact to the lives of famous people which were popular reading
for antiquarians in the sixteenth century. Publications such as
Guillaume Rouillé's *Promptuaire des médailles* (1553) and Fulvio Orsini's
*Imagines et Elogia Virorum Illustrium* (1570), lavishly illustrated with
drawings of ancient coins (which they referred to as 'medals'), could only
further promote the fashion for collecting coins. The portraits were, of
course, the key requirement, and 'portraits' from fantasy ancient coins
were sometimes invented to fill gaps and to create images for characters
(Moses, Samson and so on) from well before the invention of coinage.
Among the genuine coins, Roman imperial portraits again dominate,
but we also find Greek coins providing images, which may be rightly or
wrongly attributed. Hellenistic kings were usually straightforward –
Philetaerus of Pergamum, Prusias II of Bithynia, for example – but
sometimes coins had to be misattributed to furnish a desired portrait.
Thus bearded heads with Attic helmets (themselves based on Athena
heads from Athenian coinage) on coins from Tarsus in Cilicia from the
370s BC are imaginatively misidentified as the (much later) Carthaginian
generals Hamilcar and Hannibal. In addition to the coin portraits, these

PHILETAERVS.

*Apud Cardinalem Farnesium
in nomismate argenteo.*

69 *Illustrations in Orsini's
Illustrium Imagines: the
portrait copying coins of
Pergamum (compare fig.
45a) is correctly identified
as Philetaerus, but the
portrait based on coins of
Tarsus (compare fig. 33a) is
wrongly identified as
Hannibal.*

HANNIBAL.

*Apud Fulvium Vrsinum
in nomismate argenteo.*

volumes might also include other images from Greek coins, including, for instance, an assortment of Heracles and Nemean lion designs from Greek coins of Heraclea and Syracuse in the *Sicilia et Magna Graecia* (Bruges, 1576) of Hubert Goltz.

The more academic study of Greek coins belongs to a later age. The first serious study of a Greek coin hoard was by the German scholar Gottlieb Siegfried Bayer in 1727, and the first great scientific catalogue of Greek coins was the *Doctrina numorum veterum* (1792–8) of Joseph Eckhel, based on the Imperial Collection in Vienna. Collections were the key to study, and the late eighteenth century was a lively period for the collecting of Greek coins. One of the greatest collections formed at this time was that of Dr William Hunter, who amassed more than 12,000 Greek coins. The records of correspondence relating to the formation of his collections provide some fascinating glimpses into the world of coin collecting in the late eighteenth century. Sir William Hamilton, British ambassador at Naples, wrote to Hunter on 4 October 1774: '. . . I think these medals [coins] . . . are as fine and as well preserved as any I ever saw. . . . The owner is a gamester and a sum properly offer'd may do the business at a proper season. . . . I shou'd be glad to enrich my country by this collection at the same time that I give you pleasure . . .' Hunter's cautious reply included the following: '. . . we cannot pretend to calculate . . . the real value of a collection, by a catalogue. . . . And, among the Italians especially, men of the fairest pretensions to honour will cheat in recommending their medals, as they will here in selling horses . . .' Hunter collected for pleasure but he was also aware of the potential of his coins for 'the illustration and confirmation of history', and he later bequeathed his entire collections to the University of Glasgow so that they could be used by generations of students for the advancement of knowledge.

The invention of photography in the nineteenth century and its use in publications has been the main catalyst for the huge advances since made in numismatic study. Students are no longer confined to working solely within the great collections, and with only laboriously made plaster casts for comparative study. There are now numerous catalogues and studies, comprehensively illustrated with photographs, and computer databases with enormous capacity are also being developed.

Many of the advances in numismatic study (for example, the first published die link and the first die studies) have taken place in the field of Greek coins. Similarly, Greek coins have provided some of the best examples of the application of numismatic evidence for studies in history (political, economic or social) and art history. Particularly important are the hoards of coins now being unearthed and published in greater numbers than ever. These provide the richest source of new evidence, whether in the pattern of coinage they contain, the dating evidence they can provide, or in the new individual pieces they may yield. One of the fascinations of Greek coins is that each specimen can be a historical document, and new ones are still turning up.

The development of numismatics as a scientific subject has thus enabled the potential of Greek coinage for academic study to be exploited more fully, and today Greek coins are encountered across a wide range of publications. Entire series of catalogues are devoted to them, as in the *Sylloge Nummorum Graecorum* volumes, as well as a substantial library of general and specialised academic numismatic books and journals. They are also frequently referred to and illustrated in non-numismatic works on Greek history or civilisation, and even when their potential for providing evidence is ignored they are sometimes used for symbolic or decorative purposes in historical or other publications. Within the field of numismatics Greek coins have always held a special position, in part because of their unrivalled beauty. Their images continue to excite the imagination, a typical example being the frequently encountered Heracles and Nemean lion design derived ultimately from the coinage of Heraclea. One of its latest reincarnations is on the obverse of the new medal of the Royal Numismatic Society — a glowing testimony to the lasting appeal of the original Greek coin.

70

70 *Medal of the Royal Numismatic Society, by Ian Rank-Broadley, first presented in 1993. (less than half actual size)*

# Further Reading

I. Carradice and M. Price, *Coinage in the Greek World* (London, 1988).

M. H. Crawford, *Coinage and Money under the Roman Republic* (London, 1985).

B. V. Head, *Historia Numorum* (London, 1911, reprinted 1977).

G. K. Jenkins, *Ancient Greek Coins* (London, 1972, 2nd edn 1990).

C. M. Kraay and M. Hirmer, *Greek Coins* (London, 1966).

C. M. Kraay, *Archaic and Classical Greek Coins* (London, 1976).

J. R. Melville Jones, *Testimonia Numaria: Greek and Latin Texts concerning Ancient Greek Coinage* (vol. 1, London, 1993).

O. Morkholm, *Early Hellenistic Coinage* (Cambridge, 1991).

M. J. Price and N. M. Waggoner, *Archaic Greek Silver Coinage: The Asyut Hoard* (London, 1976).

## Further study

There are numerous studies of coinage issues, groups of issues, individual mints, groups of mints, etc. More detailed bibliographies can be found in some of the above-listed books, notably those by Kraay and Morkholm. Articles are usually published in numismatic journals such as the *Numismatic Chronicle*, the *American Journal of Numismatics* and the *Revue Numismatique*. Regional bibliographies have been published occasionally in German in the periodical *Chiron* since 1972. Published numismatic research is also listed annually in the periodical *Numismatic Literature*, produced by the American Numismatic Society, and *Surveys of Recent Numismatic Research* are published on the occasion of the International Numismatic Congresses, most recently Berne 1979, London 1986 and Brussels 1991. For the study of Greek coin hoards the essential starting point is M. Thompson, O. Morkholm, C. M. Kraay (eds), *An Inventory of Greek Coin Hoards* (New York, 1973), supplemented by the periodical *Coin Hoards* (since 1994 incorporated in the *Numismatic Chronicle*).

## Coin collections

Numismatic study requires the inspection of coins and the largest accessible collections are held in the great public museums, most of which have been published. The format now used as standard is that of the *Sylloge Nummorum Graecorum* series, in which all the coins tend to be illustrated. *SNG* series now exist for collections in Denmark, Finland, France, Germany, Great Britain, Greece, Sweden, Switzerland and the United States. There are also twenty-nine volumes of *BMC* (*Catalogue of Greek Coins in the British Museum*), recently extended by M. J. Price's *The Coinage in the Name of Alexander the Great and Philip Arrhidaeus* and *SNG British Museum, The Black Sea*.

# Illustrations

Most of the illustrations are of coins held in the British Museum's Department of Coins and Medals (CM, BMC, PCG, SNG). Other items are in the Departments of Greek and Roman Antiquities (GR) or Prints and Drawings (PD). Copyright in the photographs belongs to the Trustees of the British Museum.

# Index